The Essential Guide to Buying and Selling a Car in Canada

Kendrew Pape

Mel Wise

Prentice Hall Canada Inc.
Scarborough, Ontario

Canadian Cataloguing in Publication Data

Pape, Kendrew
  The essential guide to buying and selling a car in Canada

ISBN 0-13-080122-4

1. Automobiles – Canada – Purchasing. 2. Selling – Automobiles – Canada.
I. Wise, Mel.   II. Title.

TL162.P36 1998   629.222'029'7   C97-932775-X

Prentice-Hall, Inc., Upper Saddle River, New Jersey
Prentice-Hall International (UK) Limited, London
Prentice-Hall of Australia, Pty. Limited, Sydney
Prentice-Hall Hispanoamericana, S.A., Mexico City
Prentice-Hall of India Private Limited, New Delhi
Prentice-Hall of Japan, Inc., Tokyo
Simon & Schuster Asia Private Limited, Singapore
Editora Prentice-Hall do Brasil, Ltda., Rio de Janeiro

ISBN 0-13-080122-4

Acquisitions Editor: Robert Harris
Production Editor: Susan James
Copy Editor: Tanya Long
Art Director: Mary Opper
Production Coordinator: Julie Preston
Interior Design/Page Layout: Jack Steiner
Cover Design: Sputnik
Cover Image: Jed Share/Photonica

1 2 3 4 5   WW   02 01 00 99 98

Printed and bound in Canada.

Visit the Prentice Hall Canada Web site! Send us your comments, browse
our catalogues, and more. **www.phcanada.com**

Contents

Page #2 " HighLites"

Preface

This book will teach you almost everything you need to know about buying a car in Canada. It's designed to take you through the process step by step, beginning with the stages of planning and preparation, and following the car-buying process through the negotiations, signing the bill of sale, buying insurance, and even selling your used car yourself. There is no other book available in Canada that is as comprehensive as this one. If you need to buy a new or used car this year, you'll find this book to be an indispensable tool.

Marshall McLuhan, the noted Canadian communications theorist, once claimed that the car had become the carapace of urban and suburban people. We hide in its protective cocoon, zipping down the highway surrounded by hundreds of similarly encapsulated people. The car protects us from the world outside, giving us a hard exoskeleton with which we can deflect the bumps and bruises of everyday life. In her book *Everything Women Always Wanted to Know About Cars (But Didn't Know Who to Ask)*, renowned columnist Lesley Hazleton compares the car to a metal womb, "a small, defined space that enfolds its occupants safely against the world."

The car offers an intimate space for its occupants. Protected by a veil of privacy and safety, a couple travelling in a car will have intimate conversations that they couldn't conduct face to face. Hazleton notes: "In a car, you're both looking at the road ahead...the conscious self is otherwise occupied, leaving the subconscious mind free to emerge."

All of these elements make the automobile far more than just a means of transportation—they transform it into an extension of the individual. Great drivers such as Formula One World Champion Jacques Villeneuve will think of their car as nothing more than the shell that surrounds them. The pedals are extensions of the feet. The wheel is a tool in the driver's hands.

Buying a new car is simply the process of replacing one shell for another. Like the hermit crab that discards its home when it grows too old, so do we replace our cars.

This book makes the process easier and more enjoyable.

Putting a book like this together requires a lot of co-ordination and hard work. As a result, there's plenty of people who need to be thanked. The publisher, Prentice Hall Canada, has again gone to great lengths to make this book look great and read seamlessly. Thanks to Tanya Long, Susan James, and Robert Harris, all of whom have huge reserves of patience and understanding—necessary for working on this project.

This book wouldn't exist if it weren't for the efforts of a few people behind the scenes. Thanks to Michael Nyman—may your routes always pass quickly and easily, Mike. Thanks also to Katya Schmied for her patience, prodding and support. Finally, thanks to Gordon Pape for his advice and tireless support of this project.

Kendrew Pape and Mel Wise
Toronto
December 1997

1

Making Plans

IN THIS CHAPTER:

BUYING AND SELLING CARS. Colourful and confusing, today's automobile marketplace offers a dazzling array of colours, shapes, and features. Consumers can choose from a full range of vintage, used, or new cars. This section explains how to hold your ground against professional car buyers and sellers.

QUALIFYING QUESTIONS. Salespeople use a list of standard qualifying questions to determine the automotive needs of their customers. The list presented in this section helps readers answer these questions for themselves, away from the pressures of the sale.

CAR-BUYER'S CHECKLIST. This checklist helps readers narrow their choices and determine on paper what they want from their next automobile.

OPTIONS. Choosing from the many options available for new cars is one of the hardest parts of the job. This section outlines the advantages and disadvantages of the more popular options.

MODEL SELECTION. Having determined what you want your car to do for you, you now have to choose the model.

BUYING AND SELLING CARS

Dwight D. Eisenhower once said, "In preparing for battle, I have always found that plans are useless, but planning is indispensable." For most people, buying a car isn't a time of war, but the comment holds true. You can and should make all the plans in the world before you go buy your next car. But know that once you're in the crunch, all those meticulous plans will become nothing more than fanciful ideas. Plans and counter-plans should be shelved when it comes time to actually purchase the car you've decided on.

The importance of planning is to educate yourself about buying and selling cars. Like every other industry, the automobile manufacturers and dealerships have spent thousands of hours refining their marketing and sales practices to benefit themselves. To make the most of your car-buying experience, you need to invest time up front. Whether you're considering a new car or a used one, every hour of preparation will save you an additional $100 off the purchase price of your car. Of course, there's a limit—you can't expect to spend 100 hours of preparation and save $10 000 when you buy your car. But in general the rule holds true. If you're a beginner at the process of buying and selling cars, you should aim for at least 25 hours of preparation before making your first purchase.

QUICK TIPS

PAY YOURSELF FIRST!

To make the most of your car-buying experience, you need to invest time up front. A good rule of thumb is that every hour of advance preparation will save you an additional $100 off the purchase price of your car. Pay yourself $100 an hour in good research.

The first rule in buying a car is to get one that fits your budget—don't stretch your budget to fit the car you want to buy. This sounds like simple logic, but simple logic is usually the first thing tossed out the window when you fall in love with a perfect little red convertible or supercharged minivan. An automobile can become an extension of your personality and tastes, and can eat up far too large a percentage of your monthly income. You need to assess your financial situation, decide how much you can afford for your vehicle, and judge the value of the cars you are considering on that basis. Over the past decade, the increase in the price of cars has outpaced the Consumer Price Index (CPI) at an alarming rate. Greater public and government demands for safety, quality, and emissions controls have driven the average price of a new car in Canada to over $20 000—and there is no end in sight. Consumers need to practise active awareness, carefully considering their options and making the best deal possible.

If you are considering the used-car market, looking for deals there because you know the price of a new car is beyond your budget, you'll still have to evaluate your choices carefully before making your purchase. With the rising price of new cars, more consumers are turning to the used-car market, driving up demand (and prices) there as well. The result is fewer value choices for used-car buyers than last year or the year before.

QUICK TIPS

BUDGETING

Your monthly car budget should include the following categories:

Vehicle cost: includes taxes

Insurance: amortized monthly

Gasoline: depends on size of engine and kilometres driven

Maintenance: warranty checkups should be established when you buy the car

The total tells you how much your car REALLY costs you month to month.

How Much Ya Got?

Your first step is the most important—determine how much money you can invest in your new car. There are a number of ways of going about this.

Visit your bank. Bank managers and account supervisors have all sorts of up-to-date computer software that can tell you all the answers you need to know, but not necessarily the ones that will make you happy. If you're honest with them about your financial situation, they'll be able to tell you exactly how much money you can afford to put into a car on a monthly basis. They may even offer you a loan to finance the purchase of your new car, but don't accept it. At least, not yet. Remember, at this stage you're only researching how much money you can spend. You are not seeking the financing for your purchase at this visit.

Although visiting your bank is perhaps the most precise way of determining your budget for your new car, there are ways of doing the same thing on your own. You may have a home budgeting system or financial planning computer software. You may know exactly how much surplus income you have from month to month that can be invested in a car. Or you may have a monthly car allowance, provided either through your employment or from an established budget. If that's your situation, determining your monthly spending limit for a new car won't be difficult.

You can also determine your personal monthly "car allowance" by completing the spreadsheet below. This is not a detailed representation of your financial situation— it is a generic spreadsheet to help guide you. Before committing to an automobile purchase, we advise you to consult with a financial expert or bank official.

Monthly Income	
Expenses	
Rent or mortgage	
Food	
Telephone	
Cable	
Utilities	
Clothing	
Entertainment	
Savings	
Miscellaneous	
Total Expenses	
Surplus (Income—Expenses)	

QUALIFYING QUESTIONS

THE CAR FOR YOUR NEEDS

Knowing how much money you can put into a car will also help you to determine the type of car you should own. These two factors aren't completely interdependent, however. Just because you can afford the new Dodge Viper sports car does not mean you should buy it. The needs of yourself and your family (if you have one) have to be satisfied by the vehicle you choose.

Although the following questions may seem basic, they will help you to clarify what you need your next car to be. They will reduce the chance that you'll be tempted by a car you want but doesn't suit your needs. Many consumers end up buying a car that doesn't suit their needs partly because they weren't sure what they wanted, and partly because the salesperson who helped them didn't qualify them properly.

All salespeople are taught to ask qualifying questions of their customers to better determine which vehicles they are more likely to sell. Sometimes salespeople do not need to ask any questions at all. If you were a car salesperson and a family of two adults and four children showed up to buy a vehicle, would you show them a sports car or a minivan? If you want to show them the fast little sports car, you won't make the sale, and should probably consider a different career. Salespeople know that the better qualified a customer is, the higher the chances of closing the sale. Despite this, many purchasers who visit dealers without having first qualified themselves buy cars that they are unhappy with later. Even though salespeople ask dozens of qualifying questions, they don't always come up with the best answers. Avoid these problems by qualifying yourself ahead of time.

Here's a checklist to work from.

Who is this car for? Are you the primary driver or the only driver? Will you be transporting a family? The more people you'll have to carry, the bigger the car you'll need. If you're the only driver, and there is no family to consider, think of friends. How many people will you be called on to take for rides or trips? Do you normally carry customers or clients in your car? If there are very few people who will be using the car with you, save some money and consider a compact or subcompact. If you're taking a family of five on lengthy trips every few months, you'll want to consider vans, station wagons or other comfortable people movers.

How long do you anticipate owning your new car? Today's car market ranges from "disposable" cars, which won't last reliably any more than 6 years, to "marathon" cars, which will run happily for 10, 15, even 20 years. You'll find that disposable cars are offered at bargain basement prices, and marathon models will make you wonder if the exhaust system is made of gold. A disposable car will run well for the few years you have it, but will burn you at resale time with a low market value. Who would want to own a five-year-old car that has a six-year life expectancy? Not too many people. On the other hand, a marathon car will hold on to its value like a miser holds on to his or her pennies. But it will cost you substantially more at purchase time.

What are you using your car for? Business or family? Do you want a car just to take you to and from work in the city? Then you'll want a small commuter car with excellent gas consumption ratings. Or are you planning on taking your car on long-distance drives to Florida? If so, you'll need a car that can perform well under highway driving conditions.

Will you be driving in extreme weather conditions? If so, you'll want a car with better traction or braking systems—perhaps a front-wheel-drive car. If you will be driving to a cottage during winter months, something with four-wheel drive is worth considering. If you live in an area with above-average rainfall, you'll also want to look for cars that come equipped with superior safety systems.

Once you have taken these things into account, think about what you liked in your last car. Air conditioning? An automatic transmission? Maybe you like a powerful engine, or good firm seats. These are all important things to keep in mind for your next car.

Also consider what you didn't like about that last car. Did you feel guilty using your air conditioner when a hole bigger than Europe is developing in the ozone layer? This time you might want a car with a CFC-free air conditioner. If you're looking at the used-car market, you need to know that car A/C units built after 1993 are CFC-free. Maybe you hated the fact that you had to replace your last car's entire exhaust system after only four years of driving. This time, get a car with a stainless-steel exhaust. Did you feel a power shortage whenever you pulled out to pass a truck on the highway? If so, consider a more powerful engine. Most cars offer an engine upgrade, and you can choose among models with four, six, or eight cylinders. Displacement size (the amount of volume the engine displaces) is also a factor: The larger the displacement, the better the power output and the smoother the ride. A two-litre, four-cylinder engine will perform much better than one that displaces only 1.5 litres. Also, the more valves per cylinder, the better the engine can "breathe," increasing its performance ability.

If you've never had a car before, ask around. Family members will tell you what they like and don't like about their cars. Co-workers will talk your ears off, if you let them. There are a lot of places to seek out good, free information. Remember the source, however. Your friends probably won't have the same tastes as you do, and their advice is just that—advice! You don't have to take it as gospel.

THE CAR-BUYER'S CHECKLIST

It's important to record everything that helps you define your dream car. Using the form provided below, prepare a car-buying checklist—a shopping list for your new car. Don't think about price at this point. First, develop a detailed list of everything you want your car to have and do. This information will provide an accurate description of your needs to discuss with the salesperson. The list can be trimmed later to make the dream car fit the realistic budget.

The first thing most consumers notice about our current car marketplace is the wide range of choice in types of automobile. Your personal transportation vehicle might be a sports car or a sedan, or perhaps a large truck. Chapter 4 looks at car types in depth, covering all aspects of the automotive popularity contest.

THE CAR-BUYER'S CHECKLIST

1. Who is this car for?

2. How long will you own this car?

3. What will you be using this car for?

4. Will you be driving in extreme weather conditions?

5. What did you like about your last car?

6. What did you not like about your last car?

7. What type of car do you want and with what options? (Refer to Chapter Four for more information about car types.)
   (a) Type of Car

   ☐ Sedan   ☐ Sport   ☐ Minivan

   ☐ Wagon   ☐ Pick-up   ☐ Sport utility

   (b) Exterior/Mechanical Options

   ☐ 2-door   ☐ 3-door (hatchback)   ☐ 4-door

   ☐ Front-wheel drive

   ☐ Full-time four-wheel drive

   ☐ 2/4 wheel drive

   ☐ 4-cylinder engine

   ☐ 6-cylinder engine

   ☐ 8-cylinder engine

   ☐ 10/12-cylinder engine

   ☐ Power steering/brakes

   ☐ Automatic transmission

   (c) Safety Options

   ☐ Right-side mirror

   ☐ Body-side moldings

   ☐ Full-size spare tire

   ☐ ABS

   ☐ Airbag(s)

   ☐ Traction control

   ☐ Halogen headlights

- ☐ Projector headlights
- ☐ Fog lights

(d) Interior Options

- ☐ Air conditioning
- ☐ Tilt steering
- ☐ Clock
- ☐ Cloth seats
- ☐ Leather seats
- ☐ Variable intermittent wipers
- ☐ AM/FM radio/cassette/CD
- ☐ Centre console storage
- ☐ Power mirrors/windows/locks
- ☐ Power seats
- ☐ Sunroof/moonroof
- ☐ Cellular phone
- ☐ GPS (Global positioning satellites)
- ☐ Dual climate control
- ☐ Cup holders

OPTIONS

Once you've chosen your vehicle, you have to equip it. Negotiating the options maze can be fairly confusing. Some people think of options as just frills—cruise control, a seat upgrade, or some other fancy toy. But they're a lot more. A well-chosen package of options can add greatly to the utility, safety, and life of your new car. So choose carefully.

Many add-on options comprise high profit areas for dealers, which is why they're so eager for you to sign up for them. Once you've negotiated a good deal on a car, you don't want to throw away all your savings by buying options you don't need.

EXTERIOR OPTIONS

Body-side moldings   Body-side moldings are designed to protect your car's exterior against door dings and shopping-cart side-swipes. They are also a cosmetic feature. Most upper-end cars come with them as standard equipment, but if you're looking at low-end subcompact vehicles, you may want to pay the additional $150 (roughly) to have them added on. Colour co-ordinated moldings are more expensive.

Recommended

Fog lights   Fog lights are mounted on the lower portion of the front valance, and are designed to illuminate the road directly in front of your car in foggy conditions. They have become popular as a cosmetic item, and serve that purpose better than any other.

Not Recommended

Sunroof/Moonroof   Let the breeze blow through on a warm afternoon. Bask in the sun's rays during our all-too-short summer months. Close it up when it rains while zipping down the highway at 100 km/h. Although it sounds great, there are disadvantages. You may get sunburned without realizing it. Passing birds can also pose a hazard. Your car ceiling will be lower by about two to five centimetres if a moonroof is installed (moonroofs slide open, sunroofs pop up). Factory-installed power moonroofs can be expensive, and some manufacturers only offer them as part of an even more expensive option package. Dealerships can install sunroofs, or you can choose to have either type of roof installed as an after-market accessory. Make sure your sunroof or moonroof is backed by a good warranty, however. Be aware that some of these jobs can result in leaks and water damage to the ceiling of your car, which will result in lower resale values.

Recommended under certain conditions

Decals/Pinstripes   Make your vehicle unique and distinctive by applying stripes and graphics. Dealerships will do the job relatively cheaply (pinstripes applied to the side of your car should cost less than $50). Manufacturer striping packages are generally more elaborate, and can be more expensive. Your best bet is to buy some decals or striping at Canadian Tire (or any other store with an automotive department). Costs are much lower, and application is not difficult. Still, these are cosmetic options only, and serve no useful function for your car.

Not Recommended

Mechanical Options

Front-wheel drive   Not may cars list this as an option; it's either there, or it isn't. Front-wheel drive pulls your car along the road, while rear-wheel drive pushes it. The advantage to front-wheel drive is better control over your vehicle in slippery road conditions. Front-wheel drive reduces wheel spin and increases traction. The drawback is slower acceleration.

Recommended

Four-wheel drive A car equipped with this feature will have greatly improved traction and directional control in slippery conditions such as mud or snow. Drawbacks include a severe reduction in fuel economy and higher repair bills.

Recommended under certain conditions

Engine upgrade Usually, the larger the engine is, the more powerful it is. You'll enjoy quicker acceleration, a quieter, smoother ride, and greater confidence in passing. The drawback is that your fuel economy generally decreases as the engine gets bigger. Many cars offer engine upgrades, but after driving the same car with different engines, most people find that they aren't worth the investment.

Recommended under certain conditions

Power steering/brakes This feature is standard in most cars, but you'll still find it as an option in some entry-level cars. If you are debating whether it's worth the extra few hundred dollars, it is. Power steering allows quicker steering response; power brakes give you the luxury of stopping from high speeds relatively quickly without having to stand on the pedal. Both these features provide significant safety advantages.

Recommended

SAFETY OPTIONS

Most safety options are good buys, if only because it's impossible to put a price tag on the life of a loved one.

Right-side mirror Most higher-end cars come with this as a standard feature, but many entry-level cars have cut costs by leaving off this mirror. There are no disadvantages to having the extra mirror. Your visibility is increased dramatically, and changing lanes becomes much less stressful.

Recommended

QUICK TIPS

ADJUSTING YOUR MIRRORS

If you have two side-view mirrors on your car, chances are you're one of the 80 percent of Canadians who have them poorly adjusted. Many drivers adjust their mirrors so that they can see a little bit of their own car.

The problem with this adjustment is that it shows you quite readily what is behind your car, but not what is beside you. The rear-view mirror is in place to show you what is happening with traffic behind. To adjust your side mirrors properly and see what is happening beside you, try the following.

While sitting in the driver's seat of your car, lean your head against the driver's window and readjust your left side mirror so that you can see just a small portion of your own car in the right side of the mirror. Now, lean far to the right, so that you are almost in the dead centre of the car. Readjust the right side mirror to the same parameters as the left one. When complete, you have a greater range of visibility from your mirrors. You've eliminated your car's blind spot, and won't need to make full body shoulder checks any more when changing lanes. It takes a little getting used to, but your new mirror

adjustment is much safer for highway driving. You'll notice that when you are being passed by another car, you'll be able to see it approach in the rear-view mirror. Once the back of the car passing you has disappeared from your rear-view mirror, the front of the car will be showing up in one of your side mirrors. The new configuration shows you exactly what is in your blind spot. By the time the vehicle has passed your view from the side mirror, you'll be able to see it through the windshield of your car, pulling ahead of you.

Full-size spare   Will this feature save a life? In fact, it might—the full-size spare will act as a second bumper in the rear of the car, protecting back-seat passengers from major injury if a rear collision occurs. Sadly, few manufacturers still offer this as a standard feature, choosing instead to offer temporary space-saver spares or equipping the car with four run-flat tires (a new tire technology that lets you drive on a flat tire). If the car you're considering still has a full-size wheel well, ask about filling it with a full-size spare.

Recommended

ABS   Anti-lock brakes are the new safety feature that everyone is raving about. A computer software program controls the brakes on your car, measuring the pressure you are applying to the brake pedal against the speed of the car, and pumps the brakes rapidly to prevent them from locking. The technology allows you to steer during braking, prevents skidding, and shortens your stopping distance. The only disadvantage is that the brakes on lower-cost models may give off a pulsing sensation, which is only the computer pumping the brake.

Recommended

Airbags   Consumer support for airbags has waned dramatically during the last 18 months. Not long ago, airbags were the hottest new feature in a new car. They were being touted as the best injury-preventing safety device available. Well, a few years of practical real-life testing has shown us that airbags have a lot of problems. Most importantly, several infant deaths have occurred in low-impact collisions as a result of backward-facing child seats placed in the front of a car. This tragedy can be averted by always placing your child seat securely in the rear passenger seat of your car.

Other injuries have occurred as a result of improper hand placement on the steering wheel of the car. Airbags were designed for drivers who always have their hands at the ten o'clock and two o'clock positions on the steering wheel. Here's a question for you: When was the last time you drove your car with both hands in this position? Most drivers use one hand, or drape their hands over the top of the steering wheel. Even though these might seem to be harmless bad habits, improper hand placement can result in serious injury to your hands and arms if the airbag should inflate.

Other than the safety hazards presented by airbags, they have other drawbacks. First of all, they hog space. Many new cars have had to sacrifice their glove compartments to make room for passenger-side airbags. Second, airbags are expensive. In fact, they cost so much to replace that many auto thieves now break into cars to steal airbags, not the stereo system. Finally, airbags have limited effectiveness. Alex Law, a Toronto-based automotive journalist, writes: "Statistics show that seatbelts save about 42 of every 100 people who would otherwise die in crashes, while airbags and seatbelts combined save only three or four more." (*Toronto Star* Wheels section, August 1995.) Airbags are classified as a Supplemental Restraint System (SRS—if you look at the label on the front of your airbag, you'll see these three letters in big bold print). If you don't use a seatbelt, the airbag won't protect you in an accident. A real-life example can be seen in the tragic death of the Princess of Wales in September, 1997. Although the Mercedes-Benz S class is among the safest vehicles in the world—and equipped with several airbags—the only survivor of the crash was also the only occupant wearing a seatbelt.

We have serious concerns about the effectiveness of airbags, especially given the hazards posed by this new technology. One hopes that the automobile manufacturers will improve airbag technology to make the devices safer and more effective at saving lives.

Recommended under certain conditions

(We don't recommend passenger-side airbags, but a driver's-side airbag is a good idea.)

Traction control   This is another computer software program, designed to control the power being exerted on the drive wheels of your car. It improves traction and directional control at low speeds and on slippery roads. The advantages are most notable in rear-wheel-drive cars, especially those with powerful engines like the Mazda RX-7 or the Toyota Supra.

Recommended under certain conditions

Projector headlights   This new style of headlight offers a narrower, more piercing beam for night driving or foggy conditions. Although these headlights are cheaper to replace than halogens, they don't have as long a lifespan.

Recommended under certain conditions

INTERIOR OPTIONS

Air conditioning   Everyone is familiar with the advantages of A/C on a hot summer day. It improves your comfort, reduces your exposure to exhaust fumes through an open window, and reduces outside noise and driver fatigue. The drawbacks are the exorbitant price of adding this option to your car. As well, running the A/C unit in your car reduces your fuel economy. In general, Canadians experience only a week or two of unbearably hot weather during the summer. Amortizing the cost of a $750 A/C unit over two weeks for four summers brings the cost to between $10 and $15 each time you use it. Of course, cars with A/C have higher resale values.

> **Recommended under certain conditions**

Adjustable steering column   This feature lets you change the position of your steering column, and sometimes the whole dashboard display, depending on your driving position. Most such features are tilt only, but some offer a "telescope" feature. This option also makes getting in and out of your car easier.

> **Recommended**

Automatic transmission   This feature was first introduced to make driving easier for people who were tired of manual transmissions. Now, most cars have automatic transmission and those drivers who can operate a stick-shift have become a minority. The disadvantages to automatic transmissions are reductions in fuel economy and acceleration. They also typically cost several hundred dollars more than a manual transmission. Resale is improved if the car is automatic.

> **Recommended**

Seat upgrade   Upgrading the interior fabric from vinyl to cloth is an excellent idea. Cloth breathes easier, is not sticky in hot weather, and has a higher resale value. Upgrading to a leather interior is done mostly for cosmetic reasons. Leather is luxurious and attractive, but is hard to maintain, cold in the winter, and sticky to bare skin.

> **Recommended**

Variable intermittent wipers   This feature will allow you to set your wiper speed, keeping your windshield clear and reducing wear on your wiper blades.

> **Recommended**

Stereo   Stereo upgrades are mostly expensive cosmetic options. Although your driving pleasure is increased with the luxury of FM music, a tape deck, or a CD player, your exposure to vandalism and theft is increased, and your expensive stereo becomes another distraction while driving.

Not Recommended

(But we suspect you'll get one anyway.)

Increased storage The more storage, the better. Storage areas keep your interior from looking cluttered, provide protection for items that might attract thieves, and increase your car's resale value.

Recommended

Power mirrors/windows/locks These provide a greater level of comfort, both in security and luxury. The resale value of your car is increased. Drawbacks include higher repair costs and added weight to the car, which can reduce fuel economy.

Recommended

MODEL SELECTION

Having now considered what you want your car to do for you, you must select among the different models that fit your criteria. That's where the core of your research begins, using books like this one and other resources that are fairly easy to access. Refer to the Appendix for a list of resources that can help you choose the models of car you'd most like to own. There's a lot of contradictory information in the marketplace, especially when it comes to objective evaluations of the different makes and models available. In most cases, you need to balance public information with your own driving experience. After you've selected the models you'd consider owning, you have to drive them. More on that in Chapter 5.

Once you've answered some basic questions and looked at types of cars and options, you'll end up with a detailed shopping list. The car you eventually buy should be on this list. If you find yourself being pushed towards a model that's not on your list, call a halt to the sales proceedings and do a careful re-evaluation. Did you somehow miss this particular car? Or has the salesperson pointed you in a direction you don't really want to go? This procedure may seem like common sense, but it's surprising how many people end up buying a car they didn't initially want.

2

Dealerships

IN THIS CHAPTER:

HOW DEALERSHIPS WORK. Consumers who are aware of the relationship between dealers and manufacturers can plan their negotiations more effectively. This section also explains the dealer's philosophy towards customers and how to use that to your advantage.

PICKING A DEALERSHIP. The criteria to be considered when choosing a dealer.

SALESPEOPLE. The role of the salesper-

son is covered here, with detailed information on how the salesperson perceives the customer and the sale.

DEMONSTRATION VEHICLES. Dealerships commission and sell demonstration versions of their most popular cars. This section examines the poor value that demos represent to consumers, and why they should be avoided.

HOW DEALERSHIPS WORK

Dealerships are the proverbial middle men. They are the only authorized distributors of any automobiles produced by a manufacturer for the North American marketplace. If you are a licensed dealer, you can buy and sell new automobiles direct from the manufacturer. As a dealer, you can also take a role in the sale of used cars, but any private individual also has that right. The most bankable advantage that dealers have is that they act as representatives of the manufacturer for everything from sales to service. A dealership is a source of information for the consumer, a place where the products produced by a manufacturer can be seen, tested, bought, serviced, and sold. For the dealership, the consumer is three different sources of revenue—the sale, the servicing, and the trade-in.

Dealerships want to keep their clients through all the stages of the client's ownership of their automobile. They will invest in marketing and advertising to attract customers through the door, but they rely on their sales staff to convert those customers into clients. The transition from sales client to service client is an important one, and smart dealerships have several strategies at the sales level to ensure that the customer visits the service department, improving the likelihood of earning new vehicle-servicing business. Long-term clients are much more valuable to the dealer than unknown hard-ball customers. The client who returns continually to a dealership's revenue cycle is the most valuable customer they have. A customer who buys, services, and sells several cars over a decade or more is the ideal customer for a dealership, because they no longer need to invest in the advertising needed to attract as many new customers.

Dealers work independently from the manufacturers. They are basically shops that sell and service product—no more, no less. They purchase vehicles from the manufacturer or from other dealers for a wholesale price, and sell the vehicles to the public at a retail one. They have high overhead costs—large inventories of new cars, insurance to protect that inventory, equipment to service the vehicles, salaries of specially trained personnel, and the general costs involved with running a large facility.

And, one of your greatest advantages, they need you. Dealerships need customers to walk in the door and purchase the vehicles that are backing up in their inventory. They want to sell you a car.

So use this to your advantage. Scout dealerships in your area to see which ones need you the most—and are willing to bargain as a result.

PICKING A DEALERSHIP

Take along copies of the checklist on the following page, the Scouting Report, when you scout the dealers you'd consider buying from. Rank each of the categories from low to high. The dealer that scores the highest on your scouting list will likely be the best place to purchase your new or used car.

INVENTORY

Take a good look at the inventory of cars that the dealership is holding. The larger the inventory, the higher their expected sales volume. Dealers don't like to hold inventory for longer than 90 days without turning it over—either to a buyer or to another dealer. If you purchase a vehicle from a dealer's current inventory, you'll get a better deal.

Make an assessment of the number of inventory vehicles of the model you'd be interested in buying (for instance, count how many Toyota Corollas you see parked out back). Try to judge the approximate length of time those vehicles have been there. Look for an accumulation of dirt and dust on the vehicles, as well as weather signs (rain stains or snow/ice accumulation). Your goal is to determine how quickly the sales staff is able to turn over product. If you have the time, keep on eye on the inventory lot over a two- or three-week period. If there's a lot of traffic in and out (new vehicles showing up, cars disappearing), then you've found a dealer with a high sales turnover. Deals will be hard to make, because the dealership will take the position that if you don't purchase the vehicle, someone else will come along right behind you. A dealership with lots of vehicles in stock with apparently slow sales will be more willing to offer you a good price.

SCOUTING REPORT

Dealer:

Location:

	Low	Medium	High
Inventory			
Competitors			
Sales Staff			
Activity			
Awards			
Service			

Notes:

Proximity of Competitors

You can use competing dealerships in the area to improve your chances of getting a good deal. If you're shopping for a new car, you can get the exact vehicle you want from any dealership in the area, including those that don't specialize in your make of automobile (you can, for instance, buy a Ford from a Toyota dealer). If you're looking at used cars, you don't have quite the same advantage, because you'll never find exactly the same used car from one dealer to the next.

Find out how many competitors there are for the make of vehicle you want by looking first in the Yellow Pages for your area. Start by considering only direct competitors (one Toyota dealer with another, for instance), instead of all dealers. The more direct competitors there are, the better your negotiating position becomes.

When you scout the dealers you're considering purchasing from, note how many other dealers there are in the area. Visit several other dealers (including direct competitors) before you begin any negotiations. A good trick when negotiating is to pull several competing business cards from your pocket when pressure becomes intense, and mumble their names out loud as if you're considering leaving and seeking out someone else's services.

Number of Sales Staff

The more salespeople there are on the floor, the higher volume the dealership is. A high-volume dealership moves a lot of cars, and will often sell at large discounts in an attempt to meet monthly sales quotas. Make an assessment of the average age of the salespeople. The younger they are, the more inexperienced they're going to be. Inexperience means potential money in your wallet.

Activity Level

Visit the store on a Saturday, early in the afternoon. If the dealership is busy and "humming," it's probably going to be a good place to buy a car. With a lot of sales activity going on, management can be swept up in the selling frenzy, and may often let a deal go through at a low price simply because the dealership is having a good sales day.

Advertising

Dealers that promote sales will usually bulk up on inventory for the period when the advertising runs. Go in a few days later, and see what's happened to their inventory. If the sale was a success, you'll see a lot of vehicles with sold signs in the window. Salespeople do this to prevent someone from accidentally showing customers a vehicle that is not available. If only a small percentage of vehicles in inventory have sold signs on their dashboard, you'll know the sale was not as successful as management hoped. This is your opportunity to strike a good deal.

Sales themselves don't necessarily mean you'll get a good price. Dealerships will often advertise bargains just to get customers in the door. Don't assume you'll get a good price simply because a dealer is having a sale.

Awards

Sales and customer service awards will be proudly displayed by dealers who've won them. If there is a trophy case in the front lobby, check what awards they've received, and how recently they won them. A dealership that has a reputation for high sales and/or customer service is a good place to purchase your car.

SERVICE DEPARTMENT

The service department will tell you volumes about a dealership. Most dealers make the majority of their income from the service department—profits from car sales are simply icing on the cake. A well-run, clean, and professional service department is a good indication that you will be well treated by the sales department. The dealership will want to earn your business in the service department after you've purchased a new car. Give yourself a negotiating advantage by letting your sales representative know that if you are pleased with the price of the car you are purchasing, you will service your car with them as well.

SALESPEOPLE

Car salespeople believe one all-encompassing truth. Bluntly stated, it is this: The buyer is a liar. They have as little trust in you as you do in them. As they see it, buyers never tell the truth about their trade-ins, about their credit history, about their intentions, or anything else (except, maybe, their first name). Buyers promise to come back and never do. Buyers change their stories on a whim and treat salespeople like second-class citizens.

As a buyer, of course, your perspective will be quite different.

What's the problem? Basically, it's the industry's commission compensation structure. It's set up in such a way as to force buyers and sellers into opposing camps. Every negotiation becomes a battle, the outcome of which will determine, on one hand, how much money a salesperson receives to feed the family and pay the rent, and, on the other hand, how much of his hard-earned cash the buyer gets to keep.

The average salesperson in a new-car dealership makes about $30 000 a year. The average commission per car is about $350. Out of that comes taxes, health benefits, retirement savings—very few dealerships provide health care or pension plans because of the high turnover of staff in the industry.

For that amount , salespeople work long hours. The typical work week is six days, Monday to Saturday. There is no guaranteed salary, just what you can make in sales. Each customer seen will take about one to three hours. Appointments are made with customers who promise to show up but never do, leaving the salesperson to wait and pass up other potential clients.

And, of course, buyers are liars.

As long as the system is designed this way, buyers and sellers will be at each other's throats when it comes to buying a new car. Even though you must be a tough negotiator throughout this process, we urge you to have some consideration for your opponent. Apply some elementary rules of courtesy to your dealings. If you make an appointment, show up on time. If you have to cancel, call. Don't waste the salesperson's time on cars you can't afford or have no genuine interest in. Most likely, your courtesy will be returned and the negotiations will be carried out in as amicable a manner as is possible under the circumstances.

If your efforts are not reciprocated, if you feel you're being manipulated or jacked around, go elsewhere. The freedom to walk out is the ultimate weapon of any consumer.

DEMONSTRATION VEHICLES

A demo is an enticing deal. Once a salesperson has determined that you are going to be buying a car, you'll soon be given the chance to buy a demo. What's not to like about the offer? A demo looks like a new car, it smells like a new car, and it's offered at a bargain-basement price!

But remember how dealerships work—they are sources of information for consumers, places where cars produced by a manufacturer can be seen, tested, bought, serviced, and sold.

Demos are the vehicles that are kept at the dealership to be tested. They are an advertising and marketing vehicle for the dealer. And they aren't the good deals that they're made out to be.

Demos are cars taken from new-vehicle inventory and put into active road service. Salespeople love to sell their demos because it guarantees that the customer is buying a car from the lot inventory, which means faster delivery and faster commission. Some dealerships award salespeople with bonuses for every demo they sell. If you're being offered a demonstration model, you need to know the different types of demos you'll encounter.

STAFF-USE DEMOS

These cars are used as personal vehicles by dealership staff. It's a nice perk and it gets the car on the road where friends, neighbours, and relatives can see it. These demos are also used as test vehicles for customers when the salesperson is at the dealership. The dealership owns the car—not the salesperson. That's important to remember. *Characteristics:* Higher mileage (6000 km+), "lived-in" appearance, deeper discount.

HOUSE DEMOS

Large dealerships will sometimes commission a fleet of demos from their new-car inventory. The house lineup is usually a selection of the manufacturer's best-selling cars, reserved for the exclusive use of test-driving customers. Staff don't get to take them home at night. *Characteristics:* Lower mileage, very clean interior, high price resistance.

Both kinds of demos will be serviced at the dealership and maintained according to the service schedule set out in the warranty guidelines. This may be promoted as an advantage when you're being pitched on the car, but it isn't. That's because once a demo has been brought into active service, its warranty clock begins ticking. For every month the car is in service as a demo, the eventual buyer loses a month of warranty.

So if you're enticed by the salesperson to consider purchasing an older-model demonstrator at a discounted price, the first question to ask is how long the vehicle has been in active service. You may discover that what you expected to be a three-year warranty has only twenty-four months left on it.

QUICK TIPS

DEMOS AND WARRANTIES

If you're buying a demonstration vehicle from a dealership, find out how long the car has been in active service. You may discover that what you thought was a three-year warranty has only twenty-four months left on it.

Demos are pushed especially hard at the end of each model year. At that point, a large dealership may have dozens of these new/used vehicles stockpiled in inventory. They have to be moved out, and you're a hot prospect. Be wary. Some of these cars may have been in service since the previous fall, using up almost a whole year of warranty.

THE BEST DEAL

Dealerships will retire their demos once a certain limit of kilometres has been reached—usually about 12 000 to 15 000. Even though they might sit on the inventory lot for six months after being retired, the warranty is still active and counting down.

If you decide you want to buy a demonstrator, house models are usually a better deal. Dealership staff don't always keep their demos in top condition. Although most dealerships have rules against smoking in the car or carrying baby seats (which can damage seat fabric), these rules aren't always obeyed. House models don't suffer these problems. They'll often have lower mileage, as well.

The dealership wants you to buy their demos so they can keep their demo fleet as current as possible. But the individual salesperson has a different motivation. Selling a demo guarantees delivery from stock. That means the sales representative gets paid faster—a strong motivation in a business where commission payouts aren't made until the car is actually delivered.

Demos are attractive to a lot of car buyers because of their seemingly lower price, and the sales staff will hammer away at this point. Usually demos are priced five to ten percent below the Manufacturer's Suggested Retail Price (MSRP), depending on the vehicle's mileage and general condition. But most people don't realize that demos are still considered new cars by the dealership. The break-even price is the same for these cars as it is for new models straight from inventory. Here's an example.

A large Ford dealership puts a Taurus into active demo service for use by one of the management staff. The car is driven for four months, during which time it accumulates 6500 kilometres on the odometer. It is then retired and offered for sale at the discounted price of $18 950. A brand new model from the dealership's inventory, identical in every respect to this demonstrator (except for the odometer reading and the time remaining on the warranty), retails for the MSRP of $20 590. The dealership is offering a discount of $1640 on the demonstrator.

On the surface, it looks like the demo is a good deal. What the sales staff won't tell you is that the cost price of both vehicles is the same. The dealership paid the same amount to buy the demo model as to buy the new one.

What does this mean? Well, if your goal is to negotiate a purchase price that's within $300 of the dealership's cost, you should be able to get that same price on either a demo or a brand-new car. That's right: the same price! You'll have a tougher time negotiating that price on the new car, of course. The sales staff will put up a great deal of resistance, and will likely keep leading you back to the demonstrator. A favourite tactic of salespeople when they're dealing with customers who want big discounts is to show them a demonstrator or a used car and tell them that, if that's the price they want to pay, this is the car they can buy. But if you hang tough, they may eventually come around. If they don't, go someplace else. In short, don't buy a demonstrator.

Having said that, there are a few occasions when buying a demonstrator does make sense, although they are few and far between. If you know the history of the demo, then you are at an advantage. For instance, if your brother works for a manufacturer head office and he offers you his office demo for sale, you should certainly consider it if you trust your brother's driving habits.

Demos are also worthy of consideration if you are looking for a very rare car. A demo Dodge Viper would be worth looking at, because you know it will have seen better treatment than a demo Dodge Neon.

Finally, a demo is a good buy when you are pressed for time. If your situation requires you to replace your car in a matter of days, you'll find a faster turn-around at the dealership if you purchase a demonstration model.

> **QUICK TIPS**
>
> **DEMOS**
> Demos are rarely the great deals they're portrayed as. Get a quote on a demonstrator that closely matches the car you want, but use that quote as a target price for a brand-new car without the mileage, and with full warranty.

3

Second-hand Cars

IN THIS CHAPTER:

THE GROWTH OF USED-CAR SALES. As our economic climate has changed from boom to bust, and slowly back to boom again, a large percentage of car buyers have been turning towards the used-car market for the best values. This section examines this growth in detail.

THE PROS AND CONS. If you're torn about whether to put your money into a new car or a used one, this list of advantages and disadvantages will give you some insight.

HOW TO BUY A USED CAR. This section explains step by step a sure-fire method of ensuring the best deal possible on a used car.

THE GROWTH OF USED-CAR SALES

We'll make it as straightforward as possible: Used cars are better deals than new ones. Most consumers already know this, and a large number of journalists are now catching on to this truth and spreading the word. If you're in the market to buy a car, your best choice is a used one. Here's why.

North America has reached a state of overcapacity when it comes to new cars. Every year there is less demand, and for good reason. There are now so many cars on the roadways of North America that congestion problems are a major issue facing urban planners in most large cities. There is no room to build more roadways, so other solutions must be found. For the consumer, the solution is easy: Purchase a used car and let the manufacturers know that they can scale back their levels of production. One forward-thinking manufacturer has already begun to do just that. Saturn reported sales figures that were down 17 percent from August 1996 to August 1997. To respond to the drop in sales, Saturn has cut production at their Spring Hill, Tennessee factory by 16.7 percent. Small-car sales in North America are down by 14 percent across the board.

"Population trends favour the used-car market," says Carlos Gomes, Scotiabank economist and auto industry specialist. He claims that after declining since the mid-1980s, the number of drivers in the 16–24 age range is on the rise. Gomes says that the children of the baby-boom generation are now learning how to drive a car, and that many of them will look for their first vehicles in the used-car market. This will keep demand strong in used cars as the next two or three years unfold, but we probably won't see any significant increase in prices. An average used car today costs about $12 000, which represents about 14 weeks of average pre-tax household income. At the same time, new vehicles cost consumers an average of $23 000 to purchase, which represents about 27 weeks of average pre-tax household income. For the first time in several decades, used cars are much more affordable than new—to the tune of almost 50 percent savings. New cars represented 22 weeks of average earnings when this decade began, compared with 13 weeks of earnings for used cars at the same time.

Used cars are flooding the North American marketplace. The rising popularity of leasing as a financing plan for new cars has ensured that there is a vast supply of two-, three-, and four-year old cars. Used-car lots have swelled in size and services to handle the volume of used cars now available to consumers. Megastores have been springing up across North America, with the first Canadian used-car superstore scheduled to open in the spring of 1998. As supply has increased, prices have begun to drop. In the early 1990s, used-car prices were climbing steadily from five to ten percent a year, but as the decade has begun to wind down, so too have used-car prices.

QUICK TIPS

ALTERNATIVE ENERGIES

New technological breakthroughs are leading industry insiders to speculate that the internal combustion engine may be on its last legs. The advancements in both electric and hydrogen-powered engines have been dramatic. This fall, Honda offers an electric vehicle for sale in the U.S. to compete against GM's EV1. All the major manufacturers are developing electric vehicles and hope to bring them to market before the year 2000. But what's most encouraging are advances being made in hydrogen fuel cell engines. Ballard Power Systems, based in Vancouver, is one of the industry leaders in this new technology. Ballard stock went crazy last spring when Daimler Benz, the parent company of Mercedes-Benz, moved to buy up 25 percent of Ballard. As of this writing, Ballard has contracts with eight of the nine top automobile manufacturers in the world to supply them with hydrogen fuel cell engines. Mercedes-Benz is expected to lead the way, with agreements to purchase 100 000 fuel cell engines a year beginning in 2005. A hydrogen fuel cell engine produces power by combining hydrogen and oxygen, driving the engine on a stream of electrons produced by the fusion of these two molecules. The only waste product of the engine is distilled water. A fuel cell engine will cause no damage to the ozone layer, no carbon-based pollutants in the atmosphere, and very little noise. Additionally, the cost of fuelling a hydrogen engine is substantially lower than fuelling an internal combustion engine. Buying used cars will speed the transition from internal combustion engines to hydrogen-powered ones. This technology won't be generally available until 2010, unless the North American public begins making strong demands for fuel celled vehicles now.

THE PROS AND CONS

Buying a used car is a lot like walking a tightrope. There are all sorts of pitfalls to trap you, but you can also navigate your way to owning a creampuff with a bit of luck and a lot of patience. Used cars aren't for everyone—many people find that the disadvantages are just too numerous and the potential pitfalls are just too hard to avoid. But for a lot of consumers, used cars are the only cars worth buying. Here's a rundown of the common pros and cons of buying a used car.

Pros	Cons
Used cars are cheaper to buy. Depreciation takes an increasingly large chunk out of the price of a car as years pass. This can be used to your advantage.	Used cars have limited warranties, or no warranties at all. Depending on the age of the car and the mileage it has accumulated, there may be little or no manufacturer warranty left. Extended warranties can be purchased, but often at exorbitant prices. Many used-car lots now offer free six-month warranties on their vehicles.
Used cars are cheaper to insure. Because the replacement value is lower, insurance premiums on older cars are substantially lower than on new ones.	Used cars have checkered pasts. It's difficult to ascertain the history of a used car unless you have fully documented service records for the vehicle. You may be inheriting someone else's problems, or a vehicle that has been in a major accident.
Used cars are often well taken care of. Many used cars are vehicles that have been turned in at the end of a one-, two-, or three-year lease. To avoid penalty charges, many consumers take special care of their leased vehicles, keeping mileage to a minimum and ensuring that the interior is kept clean.	Used cars are overpriced. Despite their apparently low purchase price, most used cars have large profit margins for the dealer. Make sure you're negotiating at least 10 percent off the purchase price.
Used cars are plentiful. There is so much selection that you may become overwhelmed at your choices. But with the wide range of vehicles to choose from comes incredible control for the consumer—the ability to walk away from any deal and find another one.	Used cars are unique. If you find the perfect vehicle for yourself and have your heart set on owning it, you can't walk away from the deal and buy the same car somewhere else if you aren't happy with the price. Every used car has different mileage, different options, and different driving characteristics. Your best strategy is to keep from falling in love.

HOW TO BUY A USED CAR

It is possible (and easy) to buy high-quality used cars for less than market value, drive them for several years, and then resell them at, or close to, your original purchase price. Not only that, but by learning the system and using it to your advantage, you might even make money from your car instead of becoming trapped in a non-stop cycle of depreciation. This is not some fantasy. These are the results that homework and knowledge can bring you.

Good preparation and patience can save you several thousand dollars on a used car. You can also ensure that the vehicle you buy will hold its value for several years, translating into dollars in your pocket when it comes time to sell. Good preparation will also protect you against buying a lemon. Although dealers are adept at covering up imperfections, there are easy ways to uncover problems, which we will explore further in the next few pages.

Your first step when buying a used car is to arm yourself with knowledge. Therefore, your first stop is not at a car dealership, or at a used-car lot. It's at your local public library. Used properly, it offers all the information you need to become a knowledgeable, effective used-car buyer. Refer to the Appendix for a list of resources you might find at your library.

Used-car salespeople make their money in a number of ways. Most obvious is the selling price of their cars, which can be several thousand dollars above true market value. New-car dealerships do especially well because they are usually able to purchase used cars below their wholesale value through trade-ins on new vehicles.

Before we pursue this subject further, there are two key price points you must clearly understand. *Wholesale* is the price that a car will command among industry regulars: dealers, auction houses, and brokers. *Retail* is the price for which they will sell that vehicle to the general public. That's you. The difference could be several thousand dollars.

Every month, Maclean Hunter publishes retail and wholesale car valuations in the *Canadian Red Book*. Several different versions of this guide exist, providing prices of vans, trucks, older vehicles, newer cars, etc. These guides will form the basis of your research. They are available in public libraries across Canada.

The first step in negotiating the price of a used car is to gather as much information as possible. Used-car salespeople make their money by controlling their customers. The less knowledge the customer has, the more control the salesperson can exert. Sales staff negotiate from positions of strength. They know how much they paid for the used car and how much potential profit is built into the asking price. If you're selling or trading, they know how much your car is worth, both wholesale and retail. They know how much they can realistically pay for your car, and how to justify that offer so that you'll believe that it is the fair market value.

Your best offence is to research the wholesale and retail values of the cars you're considering, and then seek out those models at new-car dealerships.

Because new-car dealers often buy trade-ins at less than wholesale value, they can frequently offer the best deals. You can find occasional bargains at private sales and used-car lots, but nothing like the value that's often available from the used-car lot of a new-car dealership. The car of your dreams may be available for close to its wholesale price, saving you thousands of dollars. Often that vehicle can then be sold privately after a few years at a price that will be close to what you paid for it. In short, you can drive it with minimal depreciation—the biggest single cost of car ownership.

So concentrate your search at dealership used-car lots.

This doesn't mean you should ignore private sales, though. There are great opportunities to get a good deal from a private vendor, mostly because you might get lucky enough to find a seller who isn't very well prepared and is willing to sell his or her car for substantially less than wholesale value.

QUICK TIPS

USED-CAR LOTS

A used-car lot offers buyers the opportunity to see several cars at once, instead of having to travel long distances from one private sale to another. As well, there is a higher level of protection for consumers who purchase a used car at a professional lot. Such cars are usually certified, professionally cleaned, and are sold with a limited warranty. In today's super-competitive used-car marketplace, you should hold out for at least a six-month warranty on the used car you purchase. Some lots will go as high as one year on a limited warranty to attract your business. Concentrate your search at the used-car lots of new-car dealerships for the best value.

Before you visit your first lot, make a list of the cars you're interested in. Visiting a car lot is like walking into a Cairo bazaar—hundreds of gleaming attractions that can quickly confuse and frustrate you. That effect, of course, is exactly what the salesperson wants. Keep your wits about you by preparing an action plan before you go.

Several publications report on the quality and driving records of used cars. The April issue of *Consumer Reports* rates car repair records and reliability. J. D. Power, a California-based research firm, issues quality ratings on a yearly basis, which are published in the media. These sources, and others, will help you compile a list of reliable cars, as well as ones to avoid at all cost. Once you have a list of at least five acceptable choices, you can use the *Canadian Red Book* to determine the retail and wholesale values of each one. You can also make use of magazines like *Auto Trader* (see Appendix) to help determine accurate prices for the cars you want to own. Although *Auto Trader* doesn't keep track of the final sales price of the vehicles advertised in its pages, most of the ads placed are for private sales. You can contact the sellers listed in the magazine, explain that you are in the market for a car just like the one they are selling, and if it's already sold, ask the price the vehicle sold for. If you're polite, you may find this information being readily supplied to you. Tracking these selling prices will give you a much more realistic picture of the market value of the car.

Depreciation is an important factor. You don't want to buy a vehicle that will expose you to high depreciation risk. By buying a car with an excellent quality and reliability rating, you'll make the first step towards reducing the depreciation bite. Carefully examine the prices for the vehicles you're considering. You'll notice that the valuation drops each year. This is depreciation at work, slowly eating away at the value of the car.

Knowing the depreciation rate of a car gives you powerful information. You know which years to avoid, which cars retain their value better, and what price to buy and sell at. Armed with this information, you should never again lose thousands of dollars on a used car. You might even make money!

The strategy is simple. Isolate the years in which the car you're considering experiences the slowest rate of depreciation. To do this, you'll need to apply some basic mathematic skills to your search. Plot the prices year by year on a graph. Make the X axis the model years of the car, and the Y axis the price in thousands. Now plot the graph. See the fictitious example that follows below.

Once plotted, the data points can be connected by a curved line. This line shows you how quickly the car depreciates. At certain points, the line may appear flatter than others. These are the years in which the depreciation of the car is at its lowest. These are also the optimum years to own the car. You will want to purchase your used car to maximize your years of low depreciation, so make sure to buy the model year that is just about to enter the flatter portions of the depreciation graph.

There are pitfalls to this strategy. Many cars are redesigned every four or five years. A redesigned model year can play havoc with a depreciation chart, producing much lower values for the year preceding the redesign. Also, the graph produced by this strategy will be based on the average retail prices for the car you're analyzing. The price you'll pay will depend on several factors: the general condition of the car, the mileage, the price the dealership paid, and the mechanical condition, among others. The prices in the *Canadian Red Book* are averaged across many regions. You might pay more if specific makes are hard to find in your area, or if you are in a smaller centre with no access to big-city dealerships. Use *Canadian Red Book* prices as a guide, but get several quotations on similar makes and models in your area.

FORD INDIGO DEPRECIATION CHART

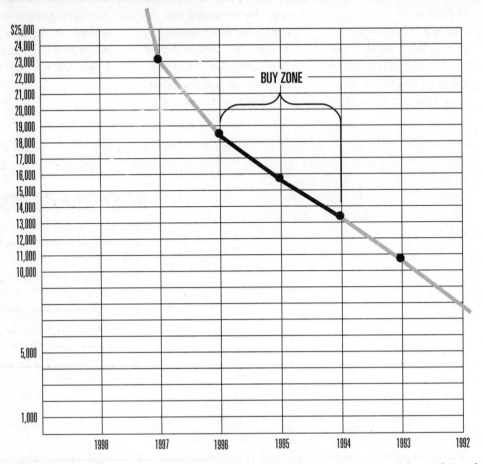

A car depreciates every year after it is bought until it is almost worthless. This rule holds true for most vehicles. Exceptions are luxury cars, which typically have a base value below which they don't depreciate much. Cars such as the Mercedes-Benz or Lexus will always retain a high residual value because of the quality of the car, the initial high purchase price, and the status value of the vehicle.

High-end sports cars have the same characteristic. Porsches and Ferraris retain their value, because of not only their status but also their limited market presence. Rarity often breeds perceived value. Rarity will also maintain values on older, vintage cars.

But these are exceptions to the rule. For most cars, depreciation follows a predictable pattern, although cars with a reputation for reliability and quality will lose value a little more slowly. Any pattern that is predictable is one that you can use to your advantage.

Once you know the pattern, you need to choose the cars. If you're a member of the Canadian Automobile Association (CAA)—and if you're not, we recommend you join—see what help they can provide. The CAA publishes regular reports on used-car quality and nominates the top used cars in a number of classes: sports car, sedan, compact, subcompact, and more.

With all this information, it's easy to determine which cars are tops in quality, and which are lemons. Use your new information to make your selections—the last thing you want to do is to pick up a used car at a great low price, only to find that it is one of the worst cars you can own. There's no point in going through this exercise to hedge against depreciation if you're going to end up sinking thousands of dollars into repairs.

When you find vehicles that match your search list, carefully examine them following our used-car checklist at the end of this chapter. Make copies of the checklist to take with you when you go shopping. Use a new one for each used-car inspection. Trying to remember every vehicle you've looked at becomes challenging after the sixth or seventh car if you don't keep a written record.

Keep track of the location of the cars you're evaluating. On the back of your checklist write down the dealership or, if it's a private sale, the name, address, and telephone number of the owner. Note the asking price, the name of the sales representative, and any other relevant details.

Do your preliminary examinations during daylight hours. Direct sunlight will reveal dents or problems that can easily be hidden by darkness. Here's what to look for during your examinations.

EXTERIOR CONDITION

Body condition Ask the owner or salesperson if the car has ever been in a serious accident. Regardless of the answer, examine the engine compartment for evidence of major repair work. Look at the fire wall, the wall opposite the radiator, and the interior of the fenders. If the vehicle has been in a front-end collision, you'll notice paint overspray in these areas. The original paint should be a dull black coating. When a vehicle is repainted, these areas are often not covered sufficiently by the body shops. Overspray is a telltale sign that a vehicle has had paintwork done to it. Look for overspray in the trunk as well. Lift the carpeting and examine the floor of the trunk, as well as the walls on both sides.

Another way to look for previous accident damage is to examine the body for rippling or alignment problems. Stand at the front of the car, either side, crouch down and look towards the rear bumpers of the vehicle. Note any ripples in door panels or fenders about halfway up the side of the body. Do the same exercise from the rear, looking towards the front of the car.

Open the car doors and let them swing shut. If they bounce off the door sills without latching, or seem to be hanging oddly on the hinges, there is a good chance the frame of the car has been bent or damaged. If the side views are clear of ripples or bumps and there is no apparent misalignment of the doors and fenders, the vehicle has probably been well looked after and free of major collisions.

Look for bubbling or blistering around wheel wells and glass, especially at the top of the windshield. This traditionally reflects the start of a rust problem. Once rust takes hold, very little can be done to stop it. It is the cancer of the automobile, and will eventually destroy the body. It can be temporarily covered by painting and sanding, but will usually recur within 12 months.

Glass   Examine all window glass for cracks and stone chips. Small cracks eventually become big cracks, and will need to be repaired. Also examine the interior fabric around windows for signs of water damage that would indicate poor rubber seals.

Lights   Ask the seller to turn on all exterior lights, including flashers and directional signals, while you inspect them from outside the car.

Paint   Check whether the body has been repainted by lifting the molding edge along windows and doors. The original paint will usually still show through. Also examine the inside edge of doors for colour distortion. A vehicle that has been painted might have rust or body problems underneath the new coat. Also, new paint jobs don't have as strong a finish as the original paint, leaving the car more prone to stone chips and scratches.

Doors/Hood/Trunk   Open them all and make sure that they work properly. Each door should shut properly with an easy push. If they bang or bounce off the door frame, they aren't aligned properly. This could indicate frame damage. Make sure that all keys work in all the locks, and that any interior remote releases are operational.

Tail pipe   Here you want to check the deposits on the inside of the pipe. The residue should be white or grey. If it's black and sooty, the car probably needs a tune-up. If it's black and gummy, the car is probably burning oil, which could mean serious problems in the engine. While examining the tail pipe, look for evidence that the car may have had a trailer hitch attached. Cars that have done major towing have had excessive strain placed on the engine and the transmission.

Tires   Make sure they are all the same type. They don't all have to be the same brand, but brands should match for both front wheels and both rear wheels. Examine them for excessive wear or damage. The tread should be at least one centimetre deep. Excessive wear could indicate alignment problems, especially if found in specific parts of the tire, like the outside or inside edges.

You can check the alignment by crouching down about three metres in front of the car and looking at the wheels. You should be able to see only the tires at the end of the car directly in front of you. If you can see part (or all!) of the tires behind, then there are alignment problems. Repeat the process from behind the car.

Check the spare tire to make sure that one is present. See if it's a full spare or an emergency tire. Examine it for wear or damage. Make sure that all tools are present.

Gas tank   Examine the gas intake for signs of rust or discolouring. Make sure the intake cover is operational, and that there is a screw-top cap for the intake pipe. Without the cap, foreign objects can get into your gas tank and pollute the engine.

Shocks   Bounce each corner of the car about four or five times, then stop and watch how long it takes the vehicle to stabilize. Good shocks will stop the car from bouncing almost immediately. Check the outside of the shocks for oil, which could indicate a leak.

INTERIOR CONDITION

The interior of the car reveals a lot about the previous owner and how well he or she looked after the car. A well-maintained interior will add hundreds of dollars to the resale value.

Passenger compartment   Look over the seats, dashboard, door coverings, and the roof liner for correct colour, as well as any tears or burns. Carefully examine the roof liner and any fabric that borders the windows for signs of water damage. If you live in an area of the country that is prone to flooding, check the floor carpeting for water damage.

Smell   If the car smells like cigarette smoke, the previous owner was probably a smoker. Examine the ashtray and the lighter. Although the ashtray can be cleaned to hide evidence of smokers, lighters cannot be cleaned and are a sure indication of a frequent smoker. Cigarette odours are almost impossible to remove from a vehicle. Once they're in, they stay.

Musty odours can indicate water damage, rust, or flooding in a worst-case scenario. They're a strong clue to problems.

If the car smells of cleaning fluid, someone has gone to great lengths to sanitize the interior. This could indicate water problems or cigarette odours.

Odometer   Check the mileage against the apparent wear and tear on the car. Look at the pedals and see if the wear on them matches the indicated mileage. Although it is no longer common to find used cars with rolled-back odometers, this form of crime is on the rise. Investigators with the U.S. National Highway Traffic Safety Administration report that odometer fraud is at its highest point in almost 20 years. You may also encounter vehicles that have had their speedometers disconnected so that mileage doesn't record on their odometers. The owners would gauge their speed using their tachometer, or by simply keeping up with the flow of traffic. You can protect yourself against this by examining all repair invoices. Look specifically at the mileage indicated and the date. If no service records are available, check the inside of both the driver and passenger door frames for service stickers or oil-change notices. These will display the date and mileage on them. Also, examine the dashboard for scratch marks or missing screws that could indicate someone has tampered with the odometer or speedometer.

Instrument panel   Make sure all the gauges and lights work. Toot the horn to ensure that it is operational. Try the radio, windshield wipers, and air conditioning. In short, try everything mechanical or electrical on or near the dashboard.

Put the key in the ignition and turn it one notch. Make sure that all the "idiot" lights come on before starting the car. If they don't, some may have been disconnected to cover up a problem. Look under the dashboard for any loose or cut wires.

Testing the air conditioning during winter months can be difficult because it's hard to differentiate between actual conditioned air and regular winter air. A mechanic can check it for you in a minute.

Windows   Make sure that they all operate smoothly, and that all power features work.

ENGINE AREA

Radiator   Unscrew the radiator cap and look inside. If you see an oil film on the surface of the water in the radiator, this indicates an oil leak into the coolant system. This leak could mean a cracked engine block (a very serious problem). Rust-coloured water indicates an older radiator that will soon need to be replaced.

Oil   Pull the oil dipstick and test the oil on it with your fingers (you can't be squeamish when examining a car). Oil that is gritty or gummy means that it hasn't been changed often. It should be dark gold to black in colour. If it is murky brown, grey, or has bubbles in it, it's a sign that water has leaked into the engine block—another indication of a cracked block.

Transmission fluid   Turn on the engine and pull the transmission fluid dipstick. The fluid should be clean and clear, and red in colour. Brown fluid indicates that no maintenance has been done on the engine. Smell the fuel. A burnt odour indicates the transmission could be in for some serious trouble.

Engine   Check the engine for any signs of oil leaks. These would appear as dark stains that are sticky when touched. Also look for signs of corrosion around the battery and battery terminals. Ask the seller if the engine has been cleaned or shampooed. If it has, make sure your test drive includes about half an hour of high-speed highway driving. Then check the engine again for any signs of leakage.

Belts   Make sure the belts on the fans and the alternator are not cracked or peeling. Pull on them lightly (with the engine off!) to make sure that they aren't loose. Loose belts are usually a sign that a component like the water pump will soon fail.

While examining the belts, check any visible hoses. Look for signs of leaks, like tape or tape residue.

Once you've completed the checklist examination of the vehicle, find out additional information by asking the salesperson or researching the car independently. Concentrate on the following areas.

WARRANTY

Ask if any basic warranty is left on the vehicle and, if so, how much. See if any extended warranties were purchased on this car and, if so, if they're transferrable and at what cost. Some manufacturers will only transfer a warranty to the second owner, not the third or fourth. Find out how many previous owners the car has had.

CLEAR TITLE

Check for any liens, loans, or outstanding debts. The vehicle must be free and clear. Ask the seller if any liens exist against the car. For greater certainty, do a title search. In some provinces, the Ministry of Transportation provides title searches at little or no cost. Contact your ministry for more information.

OWNERSHIP BOOKS

Look through the ownership books for information on how many owners the vehicle has had and the repair history.

THE SELLER'S STORY

Find out why the previous owner sold the car (if it's on a lot), or why they are selling it now (if it's a private sale). How did the dealer get it—through auction or trade-in? If you feel comfortable doing so, find out the name of the previous owner and contact him or her for information about the car's reliability.

LICENCES

When purchasing a vehicle from a dealer, ask to see the dealer's tax licence. This has two purposes: to confirm the name that will appear on your certified cheque or money order, and to ensure that the dealer is still licensed to sell vehicles. A validation sticker should appear on the licence—make sure that it is current.

Licences can be revoked or suspended for dishonourable conduct. Dealers who have had their licence suspended should be avoided.

THE USED-CAR INSPECTION CHECKLIST

1. **Exterior Condition**	
Condition of body	
Glass	
Lights	
Paint	
Doors/hood/trunk	
Tail pipe	
Tires	
Gas tank	
Shocks	
2. **Interior Condition**	
Passenger compartment	
Smell	
Odometer	
Instrument panel	
Windows	

3. Engine Area	
Radiator	
Oil	
Transmission fluid	
Engine	
Belts	
4. Warranty	
5. Clear Title	
6. Ownership Books	
7. The Seller's Story	
8. Licences	

QUICK TIPS

MORE OF MEL'S USED-CAR-BUYING TIPS

Narrow your final list of choices down to two cars. Do this on your own. Now that you have done all your homework it's time to bring in your other half: your wife or husband—not your buddies or your uncle, but your spouse. After all, this a big dollar item and you'll be surprised to find that two heads are better than one.

If the two of you need to have a chit chat, do so together face to face but NOT in front of the person selling the car. Take a walk and talk.

4

The Popularity Contest

IN THIS CHAPTER:

THE POPULARITY CONTEST. With cars, as with many things, popularity does not always make sense.

SPORT UTILITY VEHICLES (SUVs). In many ways a hybrid between a minivan and a pick-up truck, SUVs are currently among the most popular vehicles bought each year. This section focuses on the advantages and disadvantages of buying an SUV.

MINIVANS. If you're looking for practical transportation for either lots of people or lots of cargo, a minivan is one of the top places to look. Minivans were originally built on truck chassis, although their popularity and consumer demands have resulted in more automobile-based frames and suspensions.

PICK-UP TRUCKS. The top-selling vehicle in Canada year in and year out is not a sedan, it's a pick-up truck. These vehi-cles are the workhorses of the automotive marketplace—great storage and towing capacity, rugged, but with little room for comfort (although newer models go a long way towards ending that).

SPORTS CARS. The fastest production street-legal car in the world is the McLaren F1, which can easily squeeze off 300 km/h. The problem with that, and with every other sports car, is that there's nowhere in Canada where you can legally drive those speeds, unless you visit a private track. This section looks at the popularity of sports cars.

SEDANS. Ever-popular sedans come in a wide range of sizes and styles. This section looks at everything from econo-boxes to luxury liners.

WAGONS. They are competing quite well with minivans and sport utilities.

THE POPULARITY CONTEST

The most popular vehicle sold in North America year after year isn't a sedan or a sports car—it's a pick-up truck. In fact, for 1997 the number one and number two most popular vehicles were the Ford F Series pick-up truck and the Chrysler Caravan minivan. Third place went to the Chevrolet Cavalier, a small entry-level sedan.

Vehicles gain their popularity by representing good value for the consumer. Pick-up trucks, which are most popular in rural areas, are great values when compared to sedans. They come equipped with powerful engines and lots of cargo room, and are extremely durable vehicles. When prices are compared, it's easy to see why pick-up trucks are such popular choices.

But popularity contests aren't always decided by the vehicles that make the most sense to own. Quite often, consumers choose a vehicle for emotional reasons that have nothing to do with whether or not the vehicle fulfills all their needs. Almost everyone who drives a car knows what a truck is. It's the big, many-wheeled behemoth that charges down on unsuspecting compacts, towering high above the road and commanding everything around it. It's likely that this impression of trucks is what has made them (and sibling vehicles) so popular in recent years. The vantage point from behind the wheel of a truck-based vehicle is commanding and confident. The ride is heavy and secure. Storage capacity is large and roomy. Truck-based vehicles offer room for several adult passengers, improved road security, and a general commanding presence for drivers and owners.

Sound great, don't they? There are several types of truck-based vehicles available to Canadians, each of which serves a different market. A truck-based vehicle is one that is built upon a truck chassis, as defined by the manufacturer.

There's an interesting hypothesis to explain the surge in truck sales in recent years. SUVs and other truck-based vehicles have become a rapidly growing segment of the automobile marketplace. Of course, with baby boomers being such a major consumer force in North America, this hypothesis rests on their shoulders.

When the baby-boom generation was growing up, back in the 1950s and 1960s, automobiles were vastly different constructs than they are now. Think back to the cars of that era—the Nash and the Studebaker and such. Transportation vehicles were much larger then—they were built for comfort and practicality, not fuel efficiency and compact size. It was the golden era of the automobile industry, a time before the energy shortage of the 1970s that drove fuel efficiency to the forefront of automotive design. It was also a time before foreign manufacturers would challenge the kingdom of the domestic manufacturers with high quality and compact size.

The North American family sedan has seen many variants over the years, but they've all been able to satisfy several key consumer demands. They've been able to accommodate five or six people comfortably, so that an entire family could clamber aboard and head off to cottage country for the weekend with a minimum of fuss. They provided reasonable storage room in the vehicle once the family had piled in, so there was room enough for all suitcases and food for the weekend. They could handle the additional weight required for towing a boat or trailer behind, as well as the occasional canoe strapped to the roof. Finally, there was always enough headroom that adults who had to ride in the back didn't climb out two hours later with major neck spasms from slouching for so long.

Does this sound like a modern sedan to you? Can you imagine meeting these requirements in your Toyota Camry or Chrysler Cirrus?

Yet, until fairly recently, it was the mid-size to full-size sedan that satisfied these requirements. That all changed with the introduction of the Chrysler minivan in 1984—finally, people had a truck that drove like a car. This is a powerful need. Few drivers enjoy the sensations that typically come with the concept of driving a truck: torque-heavy engines, slow acceleration, heavy weight, and difficult turning radius.

What pioneered the minivan industry (and subsequently the sport utility and light truck markets) was the emergence of lighter metal alloys for use in construction, as well as more efficient engines that could generate more power smoothly and without the expansive low-end torque of the trucks that came before. This was brought about by the intensified competition from Japanese and other foreign manufacturers, as well as the energy crisis of the 1970s.

So what happened to those beautiful old sedans of the golden era? What happened to the big, roomy gas guzzlers that Dad used to drive—the same cars that most baby boomers learned to drive in? Where are their descendants?

Over the years they got smaller and more streamlined. Engineers discovered how to make a car literally slip through the air to use less fuel. Smaller and smaller they became, and along the way somebody forgot that people still had to fit inside.

Which explains the popularity of minivans, sport utilities, and light trucks today. If you visit an automotive museum and sit in the back seat of an old Studebaker, you appreciate the striking similarities between it and the Caravan you arrived in. Ample leg room. High seating position. Headroom to spare. Comfort.

If these are among the elements you want in your next vehicle, read on.

SPORT UTILITIES

SUVs, as they're affectionately called, are a relatively new breed. You've seen them on the road, and maybe even off the road. They're designed for the consumer who would never think of buying a truck as such, but who wants many of the same features. Fast becoming a popular alternative to station wagons and minivans, SUVs are tough, rugged vehicles with large cargo space. They come in a variety of sizes and price ranges, with lots of options like larger engines, shift-on-the-fly four-wheel drive, running boards, and bush bars. Consider these vehicles if you need something with plenty of room, sturdiness, and the ability to handle unusual driving situations.

At the same time, there are some negative aspects to consider. To start off, there's the purchase price of the vehicle. If you are going the route of the SUV, you'll pay through the nose. SUVs are the hottest vehicle in the marketplace right now. Every manufacturer is rushing to introduce an SUV and join in on the consumer feeding frenzy. Consider these examples.

- In 1996 Honda introduced their new Passport sport utility vehicle in the United States. So anxious was Honda to bring an SUV to market that they didn't even take the time to develop one of their own (which would have required more than three years). Even a cursory examination of a Honda Passport is all that's needed to recognize the Isuzu Rodeo lurking under the Honda badge—it's the exact same vehicle, simply licensed for sale by Honda.

- Luxury SUVs are becoming the rage, as fully loaded leather clad trucks like the Jeep Grand Cherokee or the Land Rover become commonplace on our roads. Among the new luxury sport utility vehicles introduced for 1997 and 1998: the Lexus LX450 (essentially a graced-up Toyota LandCruiser), the Mercedes-Benz AAV (All Activity Vehicle), and the Infiniti QX4 (essentially a luxurious Nissan Pathfinder). Manufacturers such as Saab and Lincoln are also entering the fray. There is already a Lamborghini SUV (of which only eight are left available for sale in North America, if you can cough up US$160 000), and we might see entries from Volkswagen, Jaguar, and maybe even Porsche.

- One SUV in a manufacturer's stable is no longer enough. Jeep maintains three levels of SUV: the TJ, Cherokee, and Grand Cherokee. Mini sport-utes have begun popping up at a number of different manufacturers, like the sports car–SUV hybrid X-90 by Suzuki, or the tempting little 4x4 runabout by Toyota, the RAV4. Many manufacturers are introducing multiple lines of SUVs, hoping to appeal to a wide range of buyers.

We are experiencing a great rush of product to market—but that rush exists because demand has been so dramatically high that it has made manufacturers sit up and take notice. SUVs are fad vehicles right now—they're hot, and everybody wants to own one. Unfortunately, many consumers are purchasing SUVs at least partly because of the fashion trend they represent.

Warning sirens should be ringing in your head by this point. Consumer fads inevitably lead to price inflation. You will pay more for your SUV than for a mid- or full-size sedan. The other pitfall is that eventually the frenzy will turn to a different subject, and the very expensive SUV you purchased four years earlier will suddenly be part of a glut of used trucks in the marketplace. You'll probably sell at a deep depreciation from your original purchase price. For your money, here's what you get.

1. SUVs offer part-time or full-time four-wheel drive. This is a great feature for many people. With four-wheel drive you don't need to worry about traversing rough terrain, like washed-out dirt roads in cottage country or snow-closed highways, right?

Ask yourself honestly, "How often will I be in these types of situations?" Sure, we experience harsh winters in Canada, but that doesn't mean you need a four-wheel-drive vehicle from October to April to survive. Any vehicle with a wide enough tire tread, good undercarriage clearance, winter tires, and front-wheel drive will get you through most snow conditions. You can pick up such a vehicle for about half the price of a comparably sized SUV. How many riverbeds do you plan on crossing during the lifetime of your next vehicle? The most rugged action SUV owners usually see is the curb barriers at parking lots, which they can drive right over when they need to park for free.

2. SUVs offer more powerful engines and torque. This gives you the ability to tow trailers or boats, as well as carry heavier loads of luggage and cargo.

But, again, ask yourself when you'll actually make use of this added power. It doesn't come cheap, you know.

Global warming is a problem many scientists believe is being caused by an increase in the greenhouse gases in our environment. The most prevalent of them is carbon dioxide, which is released into the atmosphere from a number of sources, the most flagrant being automobile emissions.

This awareness is prompting more people to look at alternative energy sources to power their automobiles. States like California have legally mandated that manufacturers develop and sell vehicles with zero emission capability. Vehicle emissions are currently the third largest source of carbon dioxide gas in our environment.

But recent studies show an alarming trend—the average fuel economy of North American vehicles has been steadily decreasing since 1987 (*Consumer Reports*, April 1996).

The popularity of SUVs and light trucks is partly to blame for this trend. These vehicles, with their big gas-guzzling engines, burn more fuel than their passenger car counterparts. Naturally, the more fuel a vehicle burns, the more emissions it produces.

This also results in a bigger hit on your pocketbook. Because the vehicle burns more gasoline than a passenger car does, a Ford Explorer owner can expect to pay almost 30 percent more each year in fuel than a Ford Taurus owner. This is on top of the higher purchase price.

3. Finally, SUVs provide better security on the road. They sit higher than other vehicles, thereby placing the driver in a better position to observe the road. It's believed by consumers that they are safer as a result.

But this is not true. SUVs, minivans, and trucks don't comply to the same stringent safety regulations that cars do. Bumpers aren't required to be at the same level of crash worthiness as those of cars. Airbags are not mandatory (and will be left off by some manufacturers looking to cut costs). There is new legislation in the United States that requires that all minivans, sport utilities, and trucks meet the 1997 safety standards imposed on cars, but they have until 1999 to do so. New guidelines for roof protection have also been proposed, but many safety advocacy groups are saying that they are still not enough to protect occupants during rollover situations.

So how much will it cost you to put a sport utility vehicle into your driveway instead of a sedan? At the top end of the spectrum you'll pay about 30 percent more on the purchase price of the vehicle, 30 percent more in fuel costs every year, and about 30 percent more in insurance. Sobering numbers!

But there are ways to cut back. SUVs are expensive to purchase and maintain, but you can trim the costs by shopping carefully.

> **QUICK TIPS**
>
> **SUVS AND BUSH BARS**
>
> Bush bars (which protect the front end and grill of the truck from damage) are being outlawed in some regions of the United States. Bush bars were originally developed for Australian use, to cushion the impact with kangaroos and other creatures. Unhappily, they are the perfect height to kill a child if one is hit by the vehicle. They are dangerous and a very poor choice of decoration for your truck.

- Choose a lower engine option if you have no plans for using the vehicle for towing. Savings: $750–$3000, plus reduced gas costs.

- Eliminate four-wheel drive from the option list. Savings: $1250–$3000, plus dramatically reduced maintenance costs.

- Avoid extras. SUVs look great with running boards and fog lights and bush bars, but they are expensive toys that perform no useful function.

MINIVANS

First introduced in the early 1980s by Chrysler, minivans are now a dominant force in the automotive industry. They are large, comfortable people movers, great for families and car pools. As the competition heats up among manufacturers, minivans are also becoming cheaper and more fuel efficient. Be wary though! Until recently, minivans didn't have to conform to the same stringent safety rules as passenger cars, and still fall short in the bumper impact ratings. If you're considering a minivan, pay careful attention to the safety features that come as standard equipment, and what options you would need to add to ensure a higher level of personal security.

The van and minivan industry has been one of the hottest growing segments of the automobile marketplace. Along with sport utilities and pick-ups, truck-based vehicles are at the forefront of an automotive revolution. The top-selling vehicle on the continent is the Ford F Series pick-up truck. Minivans singlehandedly resurrected Chrysler from death's door in the mid-1980s.

Minivan sales have been dropping slightly in recent years, partly because sport utility vehicles have been stealing business, but also because aging baby boomers are beginning to move past the stage of needing family haulers in their driveways. As a result, some good deals can be had on vans and minivans because manufacturers have invested so much money into the industry of late and need to soften their prices in order to maintain sales levels.

Many minivans are built on a sedan chassis to keep costs low for the manufacturer. The chassis is usually lengthened and toughened for the job, but occasionally you'll come across a van that has very similar dimensions to its sedan counterpart. One example is the Toyota Sienna, a minivan that was introduced for 1998 built on the chassis of the popular Camry sedan.

Sedan-based vans are often smaller than truck-based vans. The smaller dimensions mean you don't have as much storage room or hauling capacity. This also results in a more manoeuvrable vehicle, one that is lighter, nimbler, and more fuel efficient. They are also safer than truck-based vehicles. You'll find that vehicles built on a sedan chassis have better crash protection design. They are built with specifications that are similar to passenger vehicles, which must comply with higher safety standards than trucks. Minivans and trucks are now being legislated to comply with safety standards of 1997 passenger vehicles, but they have until 1999 to do so.

You will find that most of the popular minivans are hybrid vehicles using design elements from both sedans and trucks. The Nissan Quest and Mercury Villager are built with the powertrain, suspension, and steering assembly of the Nissan Maxima mid-size sedan. They also use many interior elements from Ford's truck division. Both vehicles are assembled at Ford's truck plant in Avon Lake, Ohio, and represent good value, although the Villager is the better value choice.

Minivans today are much different vehicles from when they first became popular a decade ago. As this segment of the automobile market has grown, manufacturers have responded to customer demands by making them easier to drive and more accessible. One of the best examples is the Chrysler minivan, which was redesigned for the 1996 model year, and is another hybrid between truck- and sedan-based vehicles. The vehicle design team spent long hours working to improve the specifications of the original minivan they introduced in 1984. One of their top priorities was the introduction of a sliding door on the driver's side. Consumers had been requesting this for some time, but engineers were having difficulty meeting the demand. They started with a swing-open door for the rear compartment, but quickly scrapped that plan when test groups continued to ask for a sliding door. The first sliding door designs they created for the new minivan had the handle at the back, which also generated complaints from focus groups. What consumers wanted was a practical sliding door on the driver's side with an easy-to-operate handle on the left side of the door— that is the side that allows the door to be "pushed" open, not pulled. Finally, all this needed to be achieved at a low enough cost to make the extra sliding door an affordable option.

For 1998, several other minivans offer optional sliding doors on the driver's side, including the new Toyota Sienna minivan. But Chrysler did it first.

The new breed of minivans is easier to drive, with peppy engines and a car-like turning radius. They are manoeuvrable, practical, attractive, and fuel efficient. Among the newest offerings are the Chrysler line of minivans, the Ford Windstar, the

Mercury Villager, the GM line of minivans, the Honda Odyssey, and the Nissan Quest. Older models like the Ford Aerostar and the Chevrolet Astro are outdated designs that don't stand up to the new innovations now available.

When shopping for a minivan, make sure the whole family gets a chance to test the vehicle. Your sales representative will happily accompany you to your home during your test drive (he or she will do almost anything to earn your business). Let everyone climb through the vehicle, and take them all with you for a drive around the block. If anyone is uncomfortable with the vehicle, it's better to find out during a test drive than after you've already bought the minivan.

It's not usually a good idea to bring the whole family to the dealership with you. They can be distracting and difficult to control, especially if you have small children. The excitement of buying a new car is especially infectious when you are young.

PICK-UP TRUCKS

Trucks are experiencing a resurgence in popularity in urban centres across Canada, and have always been the vehicle of choice in rural areas. They are durable, rugged transportation: a sport utility with a payload bed. Pick-ups are so diverse in their scope that they need to be categorized like sedans or sports cars.

COMPACT

These are one of the best buys available, if they fit your needs. They usually have a capable engine, excellent suspension, and good fuel economy. They will fit two people comfortably, possibly three if you have a bench seat. If you need extra room, most compacts are available in an extended cab design, which will give you two tiny jump seats behind the main ones. Adults wouldn't be too comfortable back there, but it's a good place to toss your jacket, store your groceries, or carry the kids. Example: Ford Ranger

MID-SIZE

These are great workhorse trucks—rugged, dependable, and practically indestructible. They come with powerful suspensions, a choice of engine packages, larger cargo beds, roomier interiors, and a host of options that will make you think you're buying a sedan. These trucks are popular because they give you most of the benefits of a full-size pick-up, but at a substantially lower price and with better fuel economy. Example: Toyota T-100

FULL-SIZE

These are the undisputed kings of the pick-up-truck world. They have huge engines, huge tires, huge payloads—they're just plain big. Think of them as the Clydesdales of the truck market. Example: Dodge Ram

Pick-up trucks offer good value when compared with passenger vehicles. They are an especially good choice if you're tempted by the allure of sport utility vehicles. They are powerful, go-anywhere vehicles, which provide you with a domineering sensation over other traffic. They provide the security of an SUV, give you great driving position, and offer lots of room, great storage capacity, plenty of visibility, and a strong sense of security. You can take them anywhere, down any dirt road or through any tricky situation. If you're looking for something that will plow through snow and get you where you want to be, you can feel confident in most pick-up trucks—as long as you know what you're doing.

Plus, they come in a variety of sizes, everything from manoeuvrable car-like light trucks to heavy-duty road kings.

Pick-up trucks come with powerful engines and solid suspensions. Brakes are industrial strength and seating is friendly. Many are available with luxurious appointments at a lower cost than comparably equipped sedans. Best of all, they're priced cheaper than SUVs. Many SUVs aren't even available with V8 engines, something you can equip your pick-up truck with for under $25 000 (some models).

There are a few things to be aware of if you're considering a pick-up truck as your next vehicle.

POOR FUEL EFFICIENCY

These vehicles consume a lot of gas. Because they are generally heavier than passenger cars, pick-up trucks require more engine power to move their bulk. That power is generated by bigger, more powerful engines than those you'll find in passenger cars, which adds to fuel consumption. Finally, trucks aren't as aerodynamic as passenger cars, so tend to create more wind resistance. This also increases the vehicle's gas consumption.

There are several ways to improve the fuel efficiency of a pick-up truck. If you choose a smaller engine (V6, for instance), your fuel consumption will drop. You can also cut back on gas consumption by avoiding four-wheel-drive models. Four-by-two pick-up trucks are less expensive, more fuel efficient, and not as costly to maintain. Think hard about whether you will need four-wheel drive on your vehicle. The authors spent an afternoon in July testing both four-wheel-drive and two-

QUICK TIPS

PICK-UP TRUCK TAX TROUBLE

If you're buying a pick-up truck, be aware that several models are so high in their gas consumption ratings that you will be assessed a penalty by the federal government when you purchase one new. Gas consumption tax can run as high as $1500 on some vehicles. Check the fuel consumption ratings before you sign on the dotted line.

wheel-drive pick-up trucks in some rough terrain north of Toronto. In off-road conditions, the 4x4 did have an advantage, but the 4x2 truck was able to complete the same course. Four-wheel drive should be a consideration only if you plan to travel extensively through very rough terrain, or tow very heavy objects.

These ideas will help you cut back on fuel consumption and lessen your gas-guzzler tax bill when you purchase your truck. Once you have it on the road, one of the biggest sources of poor fuel economy is an exposed rear bed. A cap or cover will dramatically improve mileage. It's an investment worth making, even if all you purchase is a tonneau cover.

Difficult to Drive

Pick-up trucks can be tough to drive, especially if you've had little or no experience with them. Full-size pick-up trucks are attractive vehicles—they tower over the road and elicit longing stares from pedestrians. They are brawny and majestic.

The problem is that they are big vehicles. Depending on the size of pick-up truck you get, you'll sacrifice a certain amount of manoeuvrability. This isn't a concern if you live in a rural area, but if you plan on using your new vehicle for any downtown driving, you'd be best to think twice about buying the biggest pick-up truck you can find.

Smaller pick-up trucks like the Dakota, the Toyota Tacoma series, or the Chevrolet S Series give you a lot of the benefits of larger trucks while at the same time reducing your fuel costs. Smaller trucks are more manoeuvrable then their larger brethren, and are more suited to city traffic. Of course, small trucks have less storage capacity, less interior room, less powerful engines, and less road presence. Oddly enough, they aren't the great value-for-money that full-size trucks are. For instance, a base 1998 Ford F-150 four-wheel-drive model retails for almost exactly the same price as a Ford Ranger XL four-wheel drive. Both vehicles come equipped with a V6 engine. Both have almost the same price tag, but the Ranger has almost half the storage capacity of the F-150. The F-150 also comes out on top when seating capacity, horsepower, towing capacity, size, and weight are considered.

Light trucks are still good value. It's just that full-size trucks are even better value.

Driver Re-orientation

Driving a pick-up truck requires that you completely retrain yourself on how to operate a vehicle. Here's why: Imagine that you could pinpoint the exact balance point on a Honda Civic parked in a driveway. With that point, you could balance your car on a fulcrum like a teeter-totter—there would be equal weight distribution from one end of the car to the other. On most passenger cars, that balance point is pretty close to dead centre. On pick-up trucks, the balance point is much different.

Pick-up trucks are very light in the rear. Most of the weight is up front, in the engine and passenger compartments. When empty, the rear is just a hollow box. Most large trucks are rear-wheel or four-wheel drive, further complicating the issue. When the drive wheels at the back of the truck try to move a vehicle that has little weight in the rear, it's very easy to lose traction and cause the truck to fishtail.

The worst example of this could be demonstrated in a full-size pick-up truck with only rear-wheel drive, no weight at all in the rear of the vehicle, and about two feet of snow on the ground. Suddenly, your go-anywhere truck becomes go-nowhere. One way around this problem is to weight down the rear of the truck—cinder blocks and sand bags do a good job. Another solution is simply to drive slower and more carefully.

The balance point on a pick-up truck is much closer to the front of the vehicle, unless the cargo bed is hauling a lot of weight. Combined with everything else, the entire driving experience changes. Be prepared for larger turning radii, a bouncy ride, potentially difficult winter driving, and poor fuel economy.

While pick-up trucks are wonderfully roomy for two or three adults across the front row of seats, the rear bench can be a tight squeeze on extended cab models. Young children are fine back there, but don't expect to seat several adults on the rear jump seats.

BUYER CONFUSION

Purchasing a pick-up truck can be a confusing experience. It may seem as though there are hundreds of makes and models out there, but really what you're seeing is relatively few models that are offered in dozens of configurations. For instance, there are over 20 ways to purchase a base model of the Dodge Ram pick-up truck (10 versions of the 1500 and 8 versions of the 2500, plus several 3500 models). You'll find that each version differs in one of the following areas.

Size of bed (box)   Trucks have either a short bed, regular bed, or long bed.

Size of cab   You'll find regular cabs (which seat only two to three adults), club (or extended) cabs, which can seat two additional people, and crew cabs, which give your truck two extra doors and room to transport quite a few people.

Length of wheelbase   Long wheelbase vehicles have larger turning circles and are less manoeuvrable than short wheelbase trucks.

Number of drive wheels   Two-wheel drive is less expensive than four-wheel drive, both in purchase price, maintenance, and fuel. Four-wheel drive gives you better traction and driving ability in tough conditions.

Towing capacity   The higher the model designation, the greater the towing capacity.

For instance, the Chevy C1500 can haul about 3400 kilos in towage, but the Chevy C3500 can pull up to 4500 kilos.

SPORTS CARS

It's surprisingly difficult to define a sports car. Many vehicles are branded "sports cars" by the manufacturer—and they all differ. For the purposes of this book, we've developed three categories.

PERFORMANCE

These cars are marketed for pure driving enjoyment. They come with powerful engines, but are priced to appeal to a wide range of buyers. Performance cars are usually horrible on gas, limited in storage and passenger room, and attract a great deal of police attention. But they're a lot of fun to drive.

LUXURY

A higher breed of sports car with an inflated price tag. Luxury sports cars have very powerful engines, boast top speed ratings, and have a variety of amenities such as CD players, traction control, power memory seats, and turbochargers. Remember, though, that luxury comes at a price.

MUSCLE

Muscle cars originated in the early 1960s with the Ford Mustang and Chevrolet Camaro. These are basically powerful engines with a passenger compartment. Power comes pretty cheap, but resale value is low and the level of quality on older models is minimal.

Why do we buy them? Nowhere in Canada can cars like this be driven in the manner for which they were built. We don't have freeways with unlimited speed restrictions. We don't have free gasoline to play with while testing our acceleration times. And most of us don't have the kind of money needed to own something that can be driven only six months a year in most areas, that has no storage space, and that can't carry more than two people.

QUICK TIPS

THE RESURGENCE OF SPORTS CARS
If you can't find a sports car that turns your crank in today's marketplace, sit on the sidelines for another six months. The auto industry is experiencing a boom in sports car development. Not only are new models being introduced constantly, but older models are being refurbished with exciting performance packages.

But for some reason, we're fascinated by sports cars. So are the manufacturers, who build these things for dwindling markets and diminishing sales, yet still find the engineering talent to design faster and more technologically advanced racers.

What's hardest to come to grips with is the high rate of turnover in this class—cars tend to appear and disappear almost overnight. In cases like the Toyota Supra and the Mazda RX-7, such exotic vehicles were around only long enough to tempt us before they disappeared from this side of the globe. The sports car market used to be dominated by European manufacturers—Porsche, Alfa Romeo, Ferrari, Triumph, and others. Then came the reign of the American sports car—Corvettes, Mustangs, the Shelby Cobra, and the Camaro. Recently, it's been the Japanese automakers who have tried to steal the throne, with supercars like the Mazda RX-7 and the Nissan 300ZX. And now, in the late 1990s, we have a fierce battle for domination, with new American challengers like the Viper facing off against technological wizardry in cars like the Porsche Boxster. Unfortunately, it'll cost you well over $40 000 to even sit on the sidelines for this battle of the supercars.

For about half the price you can get into a sport coupe. The sport coupe is a different breed from the sports car, although many people confuse the two. Coupes are usually designed for performance and practicality, which is why they're often built on the same frame as a sedan counterpart. They are not fundamentally different from the sedan, save that they're missing two doors and might have minor cosmetic changes. In that category are the Honda Accord coupe, the Saab 900 coupe, the Pontiac Grand Am coupe, the Nissan Sentra coupe, and other two-door versions of four-door sedans.

There are a few originally built sport coupes that are attractive cars to drive. The Ford Probe, Toyota Celica, and Dodge Avenger are three examples.

SEDANS

The sedan has been around since the very first cars rolled down European streets over 100 years ago. The first cars to see road service were large, obnoxiously noisy carriages that could carry two adults back and forth from town to home. The basic idea has been refined over the years, with the addition of more passenger room to accommodate families, more safety features, and more power. Today's sedans come in a wide range of sizes, designed to carry any size family in comfort wherever they're going.

SUBCOMPACT

These are small two-, three-, or four-door cars that are designed for city driving. They are usually very fuel efficient, but fairly cramped for more than two people.

Compact

Slightly larger than subcompacts, these are one of the most popular sizes of sedan. They will comfortably accommodate four adults or a young family of five, usually have adequate storage space, and offer good fuel efficiency. This class of car enjoys a large percentage of retail sales. Smaller than the mid-size vehicles, yet still large enough to accommodate a small family of five (if the kids are all under eight), the prices of these little sedans attract a lot of attention. Manufacturers have had to work hard to keep prices low enough to bolster sales, and Japanese automakers have until recently been the ones leading the slash and burn, price versus equipment campaign. Popular cars like the Toyota Corolla are now stripped down to the bare bones just to keep their base prices in line with North American products. And, just as in the sub-compact class, North American manufacturers are targeting ever higher levels of quality. Of course, this is steadily driving up the price, but so far "domestic" products are offered with better equipment for roughly the same price as, or less than, you'd pay for an "import."

Mid-size

This size is suitable for a growing family. The mid-size sedan has become the best-selling type of car in the marketplace. They usually have good resale value because of their popularity and fairly good longevity. Most models come with a large range of options.

Full-size

This class of sedan was in decline for several years, but has recently experienced a come-back. Full-size sedans are large, often luxurious automobiles that have a reputation for being cumbersome gas guzzlers. New models, however, are changing this image.

Premium Sedans

The large number of vehicles in this class is easily explained by our population demographics. With baby boomers now approaching their fifties, a growing percentage of automobile consumers are looking for high quality, luxury vehicles that offer prestige and comfort. Manufacturers have been aware of this trend for some time, and have been changing the market focus of premium vehicles accordingly.

The first wave of revolutionary premium sedans hit in 1990, with the introduction of the Lexus LS400. Since then, vehicles like the Cadillac Catera and the Oldsmobile Aurora have shown that domestic manufacturers can hold their own against the imports.

WAGONS

Most popular sedans come in a wagon form. The wagons of today have changed considerably from the hulking behemoths with the fake-wood body side panels that dotted our roads in decades past (for enthusiasts, however, a few domestic models are still available in this configuration). The stationwagons of the 1990s have to compete with minivans and sport utilities, and are doing so quite well.

Most wagons cost little more than their sedan counterparts, and on many domestic models there is no price difference. New advances in streamlining and weight reductions have transformed wagons into fairly sleek, efficient, low-cost vehicles. They will seat five people comfortably, with a collapsible child jump seat optional on some models. Consider wagons if you want the storage room of a minivan but don't want the "trucky" feel that minivans have on the road.

5

Test Driving

IN THIS CHAPTER:

WHY TAKE A TEST DRIVE?   Many consumers refuse to test the cars they are considering buying. Many others limit their tests to only a quick spin around the block. This section explains the importance of the test drive for all consumers.

THE TEST-DRIVE CHECKLIST.   A general test-drive checklist for either new or used cars. This checklist serves as a handy reference sheet for consumers to keep notes of their test-drive impressions.

AREAS OF CONCERN: NEW CARS.   This section highlights the key points of consideration when testing a new car. These points can also apply to used cars.

AREAS OF CONCERN: USED CARS.   When testing used cars, it's necessary to determine the general health of the car in question. This section includes tips on diagnosing general problems common to many used cars.

WHY TAKE A TEST DRIVE?

You'd be surprised how many people walk into a car dealership wanting to buy, but absolutely refuse to get behind the wheel! There's no way they can be persuaded to take a test drive.

It's like trying to drag a five-year-old child to the dentist for a cleaning. For most people, the more the salesperson tries to get them into the car, the more they dig in their heels.

Ridiculous!

Would you invest $150 in a new pair of shoes without trying them on first?

Would you lay out $500 for a new ski jacket without parading around in front of a store mirror and pretending to slalom when no one is looking?

So why do so many people refuse test drives?

In some cases, it's simply the anxiety of having an accident with someone else's car.

QUICK TIPS

TEST DRIVES

Salespeople in the automotive industry have a saying: "The longer the drive, the shorter the close." What they mean is that the longer they can keep you in your test drive, the less time it will take to close the deal when you get back to the dealership. They're expecting you to fall in love with the car and put up little fight when it comes to talking price. Take as long a test drive as you want, but never buy a car on the same day you drive it for the first time. Before you actually put your signature on the sales agreement, you should drive your car of choice not one, but <u>twice</u> (at least). Save the second test drive for another day.

Or the customer may be nervous about someone they don't know watching them drive.

But the most common reason for test-drive reluctance is the fear that it will be used as a lever to apply more sales pressure. You've used the salesperson's time, you've put mileage on the demo, so now you have to buy it. Of course, that's not the case. But it's true that taking a test drive will expose you to more sales pressure in most cases.

Every salesperson is trained to get the customer into the car and around the block. It's drilled into them from their very first day on the floor. Some dealerships even offer cash bonuses to the salesperson with the highest percentage of test drives per month. Why?

The philosophy behind the test drive from the sales perspective is something called "mental ownership." That's also why car dealerships are full of mirrors; the customer sitting behind the wheel of that beautiful convertible can gaze at her reflection and imagine herself whistling down a mountain highway with a view of the ocean, ragtop down and sunshine glistening in her lustrous hair. Mental ownership. It's the most powerful part of the sale.

That's why the salesperson is salivating to get you into a test drive. The longer the drive, the shorter the close.

This is where intelligent shoppers can turn the situation to their advantage: by understanding exactly what's going on and profiting from it.

Of course, you should test drive the car. How else will you know if this is a car that you would like to own? And don't just drive it quickly around the block. The salesperson, if he or she is any good, will want to get you on the highway and around a quiet residential area, down to the lakeshore, out to the countryside, anywhere where you'll establish mental ownership.

Go along with it. Have some fun. *Drive* the car. Just avoid letting the salesperson turn the experience into a pressure cooker. Stay in control. The dealership is fully insured, so don't worry about having an accident. It can happen occasionally.

Kendrew: I earned a few grey hairs and some severely chewed nails on a test drive with a quiet, little old lady, who believed that because she had learned to drive on one of Henry Ford's first cars, she knew more about the subject than anyone else on the road. It was like playing cards with someone who makes up their own rules throughout the game. She did U-turns without a shoulder check or any regard for oncoming traffic. She thought nothing of stopping in the middle of a major intersection to admire a passing poodle.

Parking involved simply finding an available space and bashing her way into it. Incidentally, she never ended up buying the car. She signed a deal, but the banks turned her down for financing because she'd written off a GMAC lease on a car she totalled. She hadn't bothered to insure the vehicle because she didn't feel it was necessary. Because the car was gone, she just figured she didn't have to pay for it anymore!

But very few people have accidents on a test drive. The main problem is that they don't know what to do when they get behind the wheel. The test drive is your opportunity to try out the car. So make the most of it.

Some consumers feel they don't need to drive the car because they drove a friend's. That may be true—but when was the last time you slammed on the brakes of a friend's car at 70 kilometres an hour just to test the ABS? A salesperson will let you do this on a test drive. All in hopes of closing the deal.

Some people say that they don't need to test drive a new car because they have the same model, albeit seven years older. A lot changes in seven years. No doubt you have. So have advancements in automotive technology.

Another reason customers give for not driving the car is that the wife/husband/ brother/uncle isn't around to try the car, too.

But there's no problem with driving the car, even if your spouse is not with you. You probably know your better half reasonably well. Save some time and try the car during your visit to the dealership. If it's not satisfactory to you, it probably won't be to your spouse, and you won't have to waste time with a return trip.

Most car-buying books will tell you not to visit a dealership with a spouse. That way you have an easy escape route: "I can't buy the car today, my husband's not here." Salespeople have learned that trick and know how to railroad a customer into signing a deal, even if the spouse is not around. Best to go together, because the two of you can gang up on one salesperson if things get too hot. It also saves a lot of time.

> ## QUICK TIPS
>
> ### TEST DRIVES II
> When you're testing a car, take an expert on the vehicle with you. Either the former owner or the salesperson (depending on where you've found this car) will be happy to accompany you. They are a source of information: everything from fuel mileage, gear ratios, safety features, driving tips and other assorted details. Ask questions; if you don't get the proper answers, you know your salesperson isn't up to par. Ask for someone else to help you, or walk away from the car and seller completely.

THE TEST-DRIVE CHECKLIST

On that note, here's what to look for on your demonstration drive.

First, take your car-buyer's checklist from Chapter 1 with you on your excursions. That, and any notes you've made about what you want in a car, will become vitally important as you get down to the nitty gritty. Keep in mind your vision of your dream car: The test drive is your opportunity to compare that dream with reality.

The following checklist is a reproduction of one we used when researching this book. Make several copies, and use one for each car you test.

EVALUATION SHEET

Date _____

Vehicle _____

	Exc.	Good	Avg.	Poor
Style				
Front-end Appearance				
Rear-end Appearance				
Fit and Finish				
Trunk Roominess				
Liftover Accessibility				
Fit and Finish				
Engine Compartment Layout				
Dashboard Design and Layout				
Gauge Visibility				
Accessibility to Controls				
Storage				
Range of View				
Front-fender View				
Rear-fender View				
Mirror Configuration				
Blind Spots				
Door Weight				
Ease of Entry/Exit				
Seat Comfort				
Adjustability				
Legroom (Front)				
Legroom (Back)				
Capacity				
Driving—Road Feel				
Handling				
Cornering				
Suspension				
Braking				
Acceleration				
Noise				

Comments

Of course, some of these categories may not apply to you. Use whatever portion of the checklist best fits the parameters you've set for your dream car. Or you can design your own checklist based on this example.

AREAS OF CONCERN: NEW CARS

Here are some of the more important areas to concentrate on.

ACCELERATION

Is the car powerful enough for you? Take your driving habits into consideration. If you do a lot of highway driving, you want an engine that will bring you to cruising speed quickly, let you pass trucks on the highway in a hurry, and allow you to merge with highway traffic before the acceleration lane comes to an abrupt end. If the car is to be used mainly for running around to malls and visiting local friends and relatives, acceleration is not as important. Be your own judge.

Many cars offer a variety of engine packages at different price levels. Try them all to determine which engine you prefer, and then see if you can justify the cost. For instance, the Toyota Camry is available in either a four- or six-cylinder engine. The six-cylinder engine provides beautifully smooth performance and acceleration, but at approximately $3000 more, you'll have to decide whether it's really that much better than the lower-priced, but almost as smooth, four-cylinder model. (For most people, we don't think it is.)

BRAKES

Don't just slow down for stop signs—really test the brakes. But make sure you warn the salesperson sitting beside you.

Find yourself a long, quiet stretch of road, preferably in an industrial or commercial area away from children. Accelerate to your normal driving speed. Don't try this at 40 kilometres an hour when you normally drive at 70. Stomp on the brakes. Hard. Then do it at least one more time.

If this is a car you're seriously considering, you want to know you can handle it in case of an emergency. Watch for things like brake fade—that's when the brakes become softer after a few hard stops. This is bad news. Imagine having your brakes fade while descending a steep and winding mountain road. Definitely not good.

While you're testing the brakes, see how the car handles in an emergency situation. Is it easy to control? Does the rear end slide out too much?

One of the best new features available for automobiles is a braking system called ABS—anti-lock brakes. This is a software program that instructs the computer in your car to pump the brakes if you stomp on them. Think back to your days in driving school. The instructor always told you to pump the brakes to keep from skidding when you're on wet roads or ice. That's what ABS does for you. Up to 60 times a second.

If the car you're considering doesn't come with ABS as standard equipment, ask to test drive one that has the system, and one that doesn't. Try to feel a difference, and then judge that difference against the extra cost. Sure, ABS is safer, but if the car is easy to control in an emergency without ABS, it might not be worth the money.

SUSPENSION

This is an important part of the car-buying process. The suspension determines how the car rides. That, in turn, influences how your back will feel when you go to bed.

There are a variety of things you can do to test the suspension. Drive the car through a parking lot and see how it responds to speed bumps. Do the same thing with railroad tracks. Keep in mind, the sportier the car, the stiffer the suspension. If you can't find a ride that feels smooth enough, consider a different type of car.

Kendrew: I remember wanting a sale so badly on a new line of pick-up truck our dealership had just received that I raved about how great this vehicle would be off-road to a customer who actually had intentions of taking his new truck into some rough terrain. My sales pitch came back to haunt me during the test drive—he wanted to try the suspension. No problem, I told him as dollar signs flashed before my eyes. We headed out to a big field and went off-roading.

In March.

The truck ended up mired three feet deep in mud. No amount of rocking would get it out. Four-wheel-drive low was equally useless. One tow truck couldn't do it. Two just managed.

The customer didn't buy the truck, but he was impressed with the suspension. And I learned my lesson about wet fields.

When testing the suspension, also try cornering. Watch for the amount of roll the car experiences in turns, and see how it handles in swerves. Like a marriage, anything that's wrong before the final commitment will be magnified tenfold afterwards.

Wedded with the suspension is the traction level of the car. This is usually determined by the types of tires you have and how they work with your car's suspension. Recently, however, several manufacturers have introduced a new technology called traction control. This system measures the amount of power you're supplying to the wheels against how fast the wheels are turning, and regulates that power to keep the wheels from spinning. This is still a very expensive technology, and not available on most low- or mid-priced cars, but expect it to infiltrate the entire market within the next five years.

Those are the major elements to test during the demonstration drive. Other important areas to check:

- Seat comfort. Especially important if you do a lot of distance driving.

- Position of the steering wheel and dashboard gauges. If any instrumentation is obstructed by the wheel, you'll run into problems when driving the car.

- Location of radio and vent controls. This may seem unimportant, but think about how much you use the radio in your car. It's important that it's within easy reach so you can keep your eyes on the road.

- Roominess. Especially important in the back seat. Make the salesperson drive while you sit in the back. She'll think you're nuts, but your father-in-law will probably appreciate a car with a bit more room in the back when you pick him up from the airport.

- Fit and finish. A car that rattles or experiences a lot of wind noise at highway speed will only get worse as time goes on. This is especially important on four-wheel-drive vehicles that you take off-road.

AREAS OF CONCERN: USED CARS

If you're test driving a used car, there are some additional things to watch out for. A used car is going to have all sorts of unique driving characteristics that will be completely different from one vehicle to the next—even among identical models.

When test driving a used car, there are a few key areas of the car's performance that you want to pay attention to. The most important is the way that the car steers. If you feel vibrations or sloppy response from the steering wheel, there could be problems with the steering rack or the wheels. Repairs to these systems can be very expensive. These items are covered under most provincial safety certification programs, so if you detect problems make sure that the seller of the vehicle intends to certify the car. The costs of these repairs should not be your responsibility.

During the test drive turn off the radio and the ventilation system, and close all the windows. Listen to how the transmission shifts from one gear into the next while accelerating. It should sound smooth and clear once the car is warmed up. If the transmission sounds choppy or rough, then you should have the car checked by a mechanic before you consider purchasing it.

No matter what you suspect of the car during the test drive, you should always visit a mechanic and at least have the car raised on a hoist before you consider purchasing it. This is a simple way to check all sorts of potential problems—alignment, exhaust, and rust.

QUICK TIPS

TEST DRIVES III

When testing a used car, remember to check out the car's air conditioning unit. Find out if it works, and when it was last serviced. If the car was built prior to 1993, the A/C unit may use Freon, a CFC-rich chemical that severely damages our planet's ozone layer. Not only is Freon dangerous to our environment, but it's also extremely expensive to recharge. Because production of Freon A/C units was banned in 1993, supplies of Freon have been drying up and costs have been skyrocketing. If the car you are testing uses a Freon A/C unit, you'll either have to get it replaced or simply not use it at all. In any case, Freon-based A/C is not an asset on pre–1993 cars.

Finally, make sure to drive a variety of cars, and don't let a salesperson railroad you into buying a car just because you drove it. If things are getting intense and everyone in the dealership seems to be breathing down your neck, just say that you have no intention of buying the car because you didn't like it. No salesperson has ever found a good response for that one.

6

The Negotiations

IN THIS CHAPTER:

WHY NEGOTIATE AT ALL? This section explains why consumers must insist on negotiating the price of their new or used car. One-price sales policies are also discussed here.

TYPICAL SCENARIOS. Two stories about the negotiating experiences of a novice and an experienced car buyer.

THE SEVEN RULES OF AUTOMOBILE NEGOTIATIONS. This section comprises the bulk of the chapter, with detailed

tips for each of the following rules:

1. Be Prepared

2. Take Control

3. Bring a Sidekick

4. Follow All the Balls

5. Don't Fall in Love

6. Stay Focused

7. It Ain't Over 'til it's Over

WHY NEGOTIATE AT ALL?

Most people find something distasteful in the entire process of price negotiating. North Americans have become accustomed to the idea that the sticker price is the price—every consumer item from clothing to food is meant to be bought at the price that is asked, no negotiating involved.

The only items on which we bargain for a better price are cars and houses.

The house negotiating process is one with which we have little problem, but that's because there is no face-to-face bargaining. Lawyers and real estate agents are the negotiators, effectively sterilizing the whole process. Negotiating a house purchase is relatively easy and non-stressful when compared to buying a car.

Car negotiating is at the opposite end of the spectrum. The process is designed to be as unappealing and distasteful as possible to the consumer. This deliberate reduction of the car-buying process to a high-pressured argument is designed to extract as much money as possible from the consumer, to make the buyer want nothing more than to put an end to the process and to get out quickly, no matter what the cost.

That is why most people pay too much for their cars. They are neither conditioned to the experience, nor do they look forward to having to argue for a better price.

There are a few dealerships that you'll visit at which you won't need to negotiate for a decent price on your new car. In recent years there's been a revolution taking place in the car sales industry, and the revolution is called "the one-price shop." At one-price stores, every customer is expected to pay the same price for their vehicle. There is no negotiating for a better price—the price that's marked on the car is the price that the vehicle will be sold for, whether it's sold to you or your neighbour down the street.

These stores are subtly different from regular dealerships. For one thing, the sales staff is paid on salary, not by commissions from the cars they sell. As a result, they won't fight each other for your business, and they won't keep hitting you over the head with the price of the car. You'll find that these salespeople are also very product-knowledge oriented—they have to be, since they don't have anything else to talk with you about, like the price of the car. You can ask detailed questions about the cars you're looking at, and you'll get better answers from one-price salespeople than you will at a conventional dealership.

The prices at one-price shops are non-negotiable. They are good prices, but if you really have a burning desire to get a better deal than your neighbour down the street, you're better off going to a conventional store. You can negotiate on "extras" at one-

QUICK TIPS

NEGOTIATIONS MADE EASY

Bob Prest is the founder and president of Dealfinder Inc., an Ottawa-based company that provides a great service to car buyers. For a fee of $119, Dealfinder will scour the country for the best deals on the new car or truck you want to buy. They guarantee a lower price for a car than you could possibly get yourself, or they'll refund their consulting fee. What's more, you're under no obligation to buy the vehicle they recommend. There is absolutely no collusion between Dealfinder Inc. and any manufacturer or dealership.

In 1993 Bob Prest successfully challenged the Ontario government about the legitimacy of automotive price "consultants," people who in the government's eyes were shifty criminals who deserved time in jail and substantial fines for the service they provide. Since then, the boundaries for consultants like Prest have shifted. Under the Motor Vehicle Dealers Act in Ontario, these businesses can exist if they meet the following criteria.

1) There is no collusion with any dealer.

2) They do not receive payment or any other form of consideration from any dealer.

3) The customer is under no obligation to purchase the car after having paid for the service.

4) The customer is made fully aware that all contract/warranty obligations are the responsibility of the dealer only.

Dealfinder has clients in every city across Canada. They will find you the best price and introduce you to the dealership offering the deal. But if you're looking for something more posh, there are full-service consultants who will chauffeur you to and from the dealership, handle your trade-in, and make you feel pampered throughout the process. Their fees run closer to the $400 range, and their services are usually restricted to a specific region, like Toronto.

Dealfinder Inc.
Nation-wide service
1-800-331-2044
Price: $119
Internet:
http://www3.sympatico.ca/dealfinder

price stores (for instance, you can negotiate to get free carpet mats), but otherwise, it's one price, the only price.

Some manufacturers have been adopting this sales strategy at all their dealerships in an effort to be distinctive from the competition and to provide a more customer-oriented service. As of this writing, both Saturn and Isuzu sell their vehicles across Canada using this approach.

TYPICAL SCENARIOS

A typical price negotiation at a car dealership will go one of two ways.

Scenario One

The customer arrives at the dealership after work, tired and hungry. He doesn't have any clear idea of the price of the new car he wants to buy, but knows what the most is that he can afford. After revealing this and other information to the salesperson, he is led around the dealership, test drives the top-of-the-line, fully loaded model, and is manoeuvred into a negotiating process he doesn't understand. His wife and children are waiting at home, or worse, they are with him, distracting him and providing the salesperson with even more pressure material. Everyone involved just wants to put an end to the process as quickly as possible. A deal is signed with monthly payments. The customer leaves, not really sure how much he is paying for the car, but afraid to ask.

Scenario Two

The customer arrives at the dealership late on a rainy/snowy Saturday afternoon near the end of the month. It's been a slow day there, evidenced by the group of salespeople playing Euchre in the corner. She is well rested, lightly fed, and has a portfolio full of information about what her car is worth, the dealer cost price of the new car she wants, factory incentive quotations, her pre-approved bank financing, a calculator, and some interest/payment tables (among other things). She picks a young, fresh-faced salesperson and asks to see the car she wants, equipped exactly as she needs. She controls the pace of the salesperson, asking for the test drive, asking for a price negotiation, and assuring the eager sales representative that she is going to buy a car today, right now (thereby fulfilling his monthly quota, or qualifying him for a special draw, or putting the dealership over its daily target, whatever). She makes her offers, knows how to keep from being confused, won't let any of the sales staff or managers distract her, and is prepared to settle in for as many hours as it takes to get her well researched prices. Several hours after the dealership has closed, management finally relents and grants all her demands, anxious as they are to get home to their spouses so that they can enjoy what's left of the weekend.

THE SEVEN RULES OF AUTOMOBILE NEGOTIATIONS

There is an often repeated philosophy that goes by the name of "the rule of 80/20." It states that 80 percent of any given phenomenon is provided by 20 percent of the participants. Eighty percent of all musical instruments are owned by 20 percent of the musicians. Eighty percent of the books sold in stores are bought by 20 percent of the book-buying public.

And 80 percent of a car dealership's profits come from 20 percent of the buyers.

This is an unspoken truth understood among all car salespeople. They're forever hopeful that the next person they sell is going to be part of that 20 percent, and provide them with their best commission of the month.

Don't be part of that 20 percent. Here are seven rules to follow when negotiating the price of your new car.

Rule #1. Be Prepared

Throughout this book we've stressed the importance of doing your homework. At no time is it as important as it is now.

To properly understand the real value of new cars, used cars, and factory or dealer options requires some insight into how such values are calculated. The arena you're about to enter is a thoroughly confusing one, made that way by your friendly neighbourhood auto dealer and his supplier, the manufacturer. They've arranged a network of prices, fees, and incentives, some of which are reasonable and some of which are thinly veiled snatches for your pocketbook. Unravelling this tangle is challenging, but financially rewarding.

If it's a used car that you are planning to buy, you'll find some good negotiating points in this chapter and refer to Chapter 3 for more detailed information.

The price of a new car is determined by several different factors, both fixed and variable.

The dealership cost   Dealerships buy the new cars in their lots directly from the manufacturer and resell them to you at "retail" price. The manufacturer's suggested retail price (MSRP) will be pegged anywhere from 10 to 25 percent above the dealer's cost, depending on the type of car you are purchasing. In most cases, the MSRP will be about 15 percent above the dealer's cost.

Consumer Reports has an annual auto issue in which they publish a decimal number called a "cost factor" for most makes and models. Multiply the cost factor by the

MSRP of the cars you're considering to determine the dealer cost. For instance, the April 1997 issue of *Consumer Reports* shows the Dodge Dakota pick-up truck with an MSRP of US$20 992 and a cost factor of 0.91. Multiplying the two together gives us an approximate dealer cost of US$19 102.72—a difference of over US$1800 that can go into your pocket!

The prices quoted in *Consumer Reports* are in U.S. dollars. Use the cost factor they provide, but get Canadian MSRPs from the dealer or manufacturer.

Factory-to-dealer rebates Manufacturers will often offer special rebates to their dealers on cars that they most want to sell. These rebates are usually in the $100–$500 range, but can run into the thousands under some circumstances.

Factory-to-dealer rebates are generally offered as an incentive to the dealer to sell cars that are backing up in inventory. These might be cars at the end of their model year needing to be sold to make room for new models, cars being replaced by a new design, or cars that simply aren't selling as well as the manufacturer had hoped.

Because these rebates change almost monthly, it can be hard to get an exact idea of the rebate being offered to the dealer to sell a certain car. One clue is to watch the advertisements for certain cars at the time you're most interested in buying. Cars that are being advertised at substantial savings are usually backed by a factory-to-dealer rebate, which is why you'll often see dealerships advertising great deals on "selected models only."

Bargaining for that money can be difficult, mainly because manufacturer-to-dealer rebates are very well kept secrets, and because they change quickly and often. One obvious way is to come right out and ask your salesperson what factory-to-dealer rebates are available. You probably won't get an answer, but someone inexperienced might reveal some valuable information.

Once you have all of these factors, you'll be able to calculate the exact dealer cost of any car you're considering buying. We'll use Canadian MSRP on a base 1997 Dodge Dakota as an example.

1.	MSRP	$24 430.00
2.	Cost factor	0.91
3.	Approximate dealer cost	$22 231.30
4.	Factor-to-dealer incentive	$600.00

Approximate real dealer cost   Subtract (4) from (3) = $21 631.30

This shows a profit margin to the dealer of almost $2800—some of which should go into your pocket!

Of course, dealerships are allowed to make a profit. They are a business just like any other, and need to pay expenses to remain in business. How much profit they make from you depends on how much you allow them.

A reasonable profit is necessary. Keep in mind that the dealership needs to pay for their facilities, equipment, interest on their inventory, advertising, and employee salaries, among other things. Your salesperson will probably keep reminding you of these things as the negotiations continue.

Also keep in mind the rule of 80/20. Someone is going to pay full price for that Dodge, giving the dealer almost $3000 in profit. In fact, 20 percent of their customers are going to pay full price for that car. In that light, a reasonable profit might be only a few hundred dollars. The decision is up to you.

Rule #2. Take Control

Knowing how much you should pay for your new car serves no purpose if you aren't in control of the entire negotiating process.

Car salespeople see an average of 2.5 "ups" (customers) a day. That means that they only get about two chances daily to sell a car, so you know that they're going to do everything they can to make a sale. As a result, they quickly become masters at trying to control their customers through a set routine that is designed to result in a sale. They are professionals, well trained to extract the highest price possible from their customers. They practise their routines over and over again, both on customers and on each other in training sessions. The only way to better the salesperson is to break out of their routine and force them to play your game.

It's a good idea to know the opposition as well as possible. Here's a rundown on how a salesperson takes control, so that you can recognize the signs.

Asking questions   By hitting the customer with a barrage of questions, the salesperson assumes the dominant role in the relationship. The questions will keep you off guard, forcing you to respond to them instead of coming up with your own. This is not only a psychological ploy, but also forces you to reveal information that you might not be ready to let out. The best way to counter this is to ask questions as well. Answer the salesperson's questions with questions of your own, and don't answer questions if you don't want to give out the information that is being sought. When asking your own questions, keep in mind that you are achieving two purposes: You are keeping the balance of control on your side, and you are learning more about the vehicle. Don't be afraid to ask technical questions about the cars. Your salesperson is supposed to be an expert on the vehicles he is showing you. Test his knowledge!

Making you wait   Using this technique, the salesperson puts you in a submissive position and makes it easier to control you. She might do this by constantly leaving the negotiations to "check inventory," or "confirm your financing credit." Don't stand for it. Every time that she leaves, you should leave too. Take a stroll around the showroom.

FIGURE 6.1   SAMPLE WORKSHEET

Name

_____

Date

_____

Model

_____

Equipment

_____
_____
_____
_____
_____
_____
_____
_____
_____
_____
_____
_____
_____
_____

Delivery date

_____

MSRP

_____

Purchaser's initials

_____

MSRP	Customer Offer
Sales Price	**Trade Info**

Go visit the service department. Step outside to look at the used cars. She'll come back to find an empty office, and worry that she's lost her customer. She'll also lose control in the eyes of her managers. Finally, it will make her wary of leaving again.

Writing it down   For some reason, we all attach more credibility to things that are written down. While Kendrew worked as a salesperson, the managers insisted that he (and the rest of the sales staff) write the full list price of the car at least three times on the customer's worksheets before discussing discounts. That way, the dealership's "numbers" had more perceived power behind them than the customer's offer.

It's a psychological ploy that works well, but can also be easily countered. Keep your own worksheet, with your numbers written down beside theirs. That will help you keep track of what the offers and counter-offers are, and will add more weight to your figures.

Worksheets   Worksheets are one of the best controlling tools at the salesperson's disposal. A sample sheet is reproduced in Figure 6.1. The purpose behind the worksheet is to encourage the customer to share information with the salesperson, which will be written down. Take a close look at Figure 6.1. Notice the similarities between this worksheet and the bill of sale (in Chapter 10). The worksheet includes buyer information, code numbers and serial numbers of the car being considered, equipment, list price, and a section for negotiation.

At some dealerships, every customer gets put on a worksheet, even if they just came in to pick up a brochure. They aren't legally binding documents, but are powerful tools for making the step from negotiating to buying.

Pay close attention to the equipment section of the worksheet. A good salesperson will completely fill this section, even if the car in question is a base model with no options. The point here is to build value in the eyes of the customer so that the dealership can be justified in asking the full list price, or close to it, during negotiations.

The best way to counter the worksheet is to use one of your own during negotiations. If you're only picking up brochures and are forced onto a worksheet, then walk out. Don't fill out a worksheet if you're not planning on working.

The Yes... Yes... Yes...   This is a fairly old variation of the Asking Questions ploy, but for some reason it's still around. The salesperson asks you several questions to which the only answer is yes, thereby getting you used to agreeing with him:

"You do like this colour, don't you?"

"You do want a four-door sedan, don't you?"

Then when he starts asking you the harder questions ("Will you buy this car at full price?"), you'll find it harder to say no. The way to counter this approach is to be difficult. Respond with a few "maybes," and try turning it around:

"You do want to sell a car today, don't you?"

"You do want to sell one to me, don't you?"

"Then you'll give me the price I want, won't you?"

Salespeople have many more techniques to control you throughout the sale. But you can't be controlled unless you let yourself be controlled. If you ever feel that you are losing control of a negotiation, do something completely unpredictable. Walk away, or start becoming aggressive. Just keep in mind that without you, there would be no car sale. The dealership might have the advantage of making you come to them, but you have the money they want, you have the power to leave, and therefore you have the ability to completely control the procedure.

One final note on control: The longer you are at the dealership, the more control you have. If the salesperson has invested several hours with you, then she will be more anxious to make the sale and will bow to your demands much more easily than if she's only been with you 10 minutes and still has the chance of seeing another customer before the end of the day. This is only true of salespeople who work for commission. Salaried salespeople, who represent a small but growing percentage of the total number of salespeople, won't feel the same pressure to make a deal.

> **QUICK TIPS**
>
> **CONTROLLING THE SALE**
> Salespeople see an average of only two customers a day. Use that to your advantage to control the sale.

Rule #3. Bring a Sidekick

Your sidekick will be one of your most valuable tools during negotiations. Sidekicks have several uses. First, they serve to confuse the salesperson, which works to your advantage. The salesperson won't concern themselves too much with your "friend," knowing that friends are usually along just for company, but don't have any say in the final purchasing decision.

Your "friend" will play a slightly different role. It helps if they enjoy acting. Their instructions are quite simple: Cause a limited amount of disruption during times of peak stress, and don't let you fall in love (rule #5).

When the pressure upon you is strongest, and don't doubt that it won't happen, your sidekick will leap into the fray with disarming questions like "Are you sure this car doesn't come in orange?" or dramatic exclamations like "WHAT!!! $20 000 for THAT car?!?" Your stress load will be lightened. You might even enjoy watching your sidekick bewilder the sales staff.

Give them specific instructions not to let you fall in love. Your sidekick can be an emergency lifeline if this should happen. Tell your sidekick exactly what car you want before you go in. If your salesperson gets you drooling over a beautiful little convertible when you really wanted a sedan, your sidekick will be able to drag you out of there until you've had a chance to think it through. Chances are good that the

> **QUICK TIPS**
>
> **YOUR SIDEKICK**
> A sidekick will disrupt a salesperson's attempts to pressure you. They will also keep you from falling in love.

convertible will still be there tomorrow if you decide you really want it, but at least you've had the night to think about it, thanks to your sidekick.

RULE #4. FOLLOW ALL THE BALLS

Salespeople are good at confusing the customer by breaking a deal into several parts, and then juggling them quickly so that it's difficult to keep track of what you're paying and why.

> Ball # 1: the price of your new car.
>
> Ball # 2: the price of your trade-in.
>
> Ball #3: the financing interest rate.

There are a number of ways to follow the balls. You can either remove some of them from the act, or you can keep notes on where each one is.

Too many people buy a car while watching only one of these balls. The salesperson wants to make profit in all three areas, but will happily sacrifice one of them if it means profit on the other two. As a result, many consumers think they got a great deal because they got their new car below list price, or because they got a great deal on their old car, or because they got financing at two percent. They didn't watch all the balls, however, and likely got fleeced in the other areas.

You can remove some of the balls from the picture by arranging your own financing (see Chapter 7), or by selling your old car yourself (see Chapter 13), or both. The more balls you take out of the salesperson's hands, the easier it will be to keep track of what's left.

If you decide to leave all three balls with the salesperson, then be prepared to keep close tabs on what's happening. Write down what the offers and counter-offers are. Keep a running tab on what each ball is worth. Continually ask the salesperson to clarify exactly how much the new car price is set at, and what the trade-in offer is pegged at.

QUICK TIPS

FOLLOW ALL THE BALLS
Either take the balls out of the salesperson's hands, or keep careful notes on where each ball is and how much it is worth.

Many dealerships will try to negotiate on the difference between the price being offered for the old car and the asking price for the new one. That way, negotiations are easier for the dealer, involve only one figure instead of two, and the actual number being negotiated is a relatively small one, making it easier to keep the offers and counter-offers low. After all, $3000 off of a $7000 figure seems ludicrous, but makes sense if you're in fact asking for $2500 off the $20 000 sticker price of the new car and $500 more on top of their offer of $13 000 for your old car. Insist on keeping all the numbers separate. If they refuse, find another dealer.

Rule #5. Don't Fall in Love

The old saying that love is blind is particularly true when applied to buying a new car. All too often consumers will fall in love with a particular vehicle, or even a dealership or salesperson, and allow their judgment to be clouded by their emotions. It's hard to be strong and aloof when you feel emotionally attached to something or someone. Sales staff know this. That's why they'll try to be your "friend," because they know that it will only help them in the end.

One of your strengths in any negotiating position is your ability to walk away from a deal if it is not what you want. Negotiating will only benefit you if you are negotiating from power, either real or artificial. When you visit a car dealership, your best strength from beginning to end is your ability to leave. With that in mind, don't do anything that will compromise that strength.

Don't fall in love.

Think of each dealership as an individual shop, and each salesperson as exactly that, a salesperson. You don't want to know too much about them, and vice versa. The more personal information that changes hands, the stronger the bond that grows between you. If each dealership is simply a store filled with salespeople, then the ability to move from one to another looking for the best price becomes that much easier.

Even if you do develop a certain affinity towards a specific dealer, don't let that become a reason for paying a premium for a new car. Give them the opportunity to match the best price you've gotten elsewhere, but that's it.

The majority of dealers will be thinking about the dollar profit before they think about your personal concerns. That's how they've stayed in business. Treat them similarly: Your dollar should be a higher priority then their well-being.

You've probably heard of the "Bait and Switch." It's a sales trick that you'll still find today, in which customers are lured into a store by a seemingly good deal, and are then convinced to buy something else (which usually isn't a good deal, at least for the consumer).

Although the trick is no longer in wide practice, thanks to consumer protection organizations, it is still possible to come across salespeople who will use a simplified "Bait and Switch" to sell you a car that you don't need.

Car dealerships are conducive to falling in love. All the jazziest cars are on display in the showroom, beautifully waxed and inviting you to sit inside. Mirrors adorning the walls let you see yourself behind the wheel of the sport coupe of your dreams. Salespeople are all too accommodating when you muse about possibly just trying one out on the open road—and they can do magic with monthly payment figures that leave them with plenty of profit while still coming close to your budget.

They probably won't do it deliberately, and they certainly won't do it out of malice. But they know that it's easier to sell a car on emotion than practicality, and will take advantage of that if you let them. Chances are good that there are higher dealership or manufacturer bonuses for sales staff on sports cars than on bread-and-butter sedans.

Don't fall in love. You know what car you came in looking for—don't let yourself be swayed from that. Resist the impulse to test anything other than the car you've come in for. Don't let the salesperson talk you into sitting in the newest coupe in the showroom while you're waiting for him to get a car for test driving. And bring along a sidekick with explicit instructions not to let you buy anything other than the car you're going to look at.

If, despite all these warnings, you do fall in love, walk away. Take an evening to think about it before you sign any sales agreements. The car will still be there 24 hours later.

Rule #6. Stay Focused

Distractions abound at dealerships. Other salespeople are making deals all around you. New cars shine prettily on the showroom floor. Managers walk in and out of your little cubicle with fresh smiles and happy counter-offers. And your friendly salesperson will constantly be throwing alternatives at you to test your "selection" and maybe sweet-talk you into a better commission.

You will encounter many different distractions designed specifically to remove you from more of your money. Here's a run-down on some of the more popular ones to watch for.

The salesperson switch   If you're pushing hard for a serious discount, you will almost certainly run into this scenario. If you don't, it's because either the salesperson is seasoned enough that management believes he can handle you without any help, or you're paying too much for your car. In either case, watch out.

Imagine this "switch" as a tag-team approach geared to grind you down. When one team feels they are getting nowhere, and the deliberations haven't been going well, they'll "tag" someone else to come in and take over. Usually it will be someone in management, but it can easily be some other salesperson who might have a few more years of experience. They'll come into the picture completely briefed on what has been going on for the last hour or so, fully aware of what offers and counter-offers have been made, and instructed to close the deal, ideally after extracting more money from you.

The only good thing about the salesperson switch is that it means you're close to the end. Management is ready to close this deal and is sending in a new face in hopes that they can talk a bit more money out of you.

The philosophy behind this is apparent: A new, fresh face replaces the old salesperson, ready to continue the barrage on you, while you have been struggling for several hours and are reaching the end of your stamina.

How do you counteract? Refuse to let the switch happen. Inform the new face that you will only continue negotiations with the first salesperson, otherwise there will be no deal. Back this up by getting out of your chair and preparing to leave. They'll send the old troops back in.

Your other option is to pull a switch on them. Let your spouse take over the negotiations now, while you go and get some fresh air.

The taking of the keys
This is a distraction designed to keep you in the dealership against your will, as well as provide a source of concern that will increase your stress levels and wear you down more quickly. It doesn't have to involve your keys, it can just as easily be your credit card or your coat. The salesperson will refuse to give these articles back, effectively preventing you from leaving until a deal is signed.

This can happen in a number of ways. You might surrender your car keys to have your trade-in appraised. Quite often, you won't get them back until after the deal is signed. Those keys will sit on the manager's desk until they're ready to let you leave.

If you're planning on having the dealer appraise your vehicle, bring along a second set of keys to the car. Give them just the car key, keep your other keys to yourself. If they won't let you leave, use your spare key and leave anyway.

Another favourite trick is to ask for a credit card or cash from you when you make an offer. This is described as "commitment money," to show the managers that you are actually prepared to purchase this car if the deal meets your approval. What they really want is something they can hold onto to ensure you don't leave. When they have your car keys and your credit card sitting on their desk, they know that you aren't going anywhere.

Don't let this happen. If they want a commitment that you will purchase this car if the deal is acceptable, offer them a handshake. If they won't take your word as your bond, then they obviously don't have customer service as their first priority, and won't be the dealer you want to build a relationship with.

The "Let me show you something else."
You'll often run into salespeople who will use this tool because it is a very effective way of pulling extra money out of customers. Let's say you wanted to buy a new Toyota Corolla listing at $14 128 +++ (+++ is industry lingo for plus freight, plus taxes, plus licensing... etc.). You offer $12 200 +++, take it or leave it.

The salesperson might pull the "Let me show you something else" trick by leading you out to the used-car lot and showing you a mildly used 1996 Corolla listing at $12 500.

"If that's how much you want to spend," he'll say, "this is the car you can buy."

You can substitute a demonstrator vehicle, a model with less equipment, or a less expensive make of car for the used one. The purpose of the trick is to build vehicle value in the eyes of the customer, and shock them with the prospect that they might not get what they want.

Of course, this trick is most effective on people who haven't done their research into the prices of the cars they want to buy. However, no matter what your level of preparedness might be, chances are good that you'll run into some form of this trick.

The underlying premise to this entire section is not to let yourself be distracted. Don't let the salesperson talk you into another car. Don't let them switch sales staff on you. Don't let the "inventory control manager" sit down with you to have a chat about the price of the car. Don't let them sell you options and equipment you don't need. Keep to your written description of the car and the price range you will pay for it.

RULE #7. IT AIN'T OVER 'TIL IT'S OVER

This rule is probably a familiar one. It applies to sporting events, social gatherings, entertainment—practically anything. The crowds heading for the exits in the ninth inning of the baseball game will miss the wild pitch that allows the home team to score the tying run and then win the game in the tenth. Guests who leave the party early invariably miss the host donning a lampshade and belting out "Feelings" to the boss's wife.

It seems to be a general law of nature that those of us who tune out before the final act is finished usually miss something of great importance. The same will happen when you're buying your next car.

After all the hours of negotiating and test driving, offers and counter-offers, the final act is often played out to customers who have eased into a contented reverie and lose the whole ball of wax in the process.

Until a legal agreement is signed by both you and a representative from the dealership, do not relax your guard. Stay alert and aware, because the moment when everything can become completely undone is when you are in the "financing" office and the "business manager" begins his spiel about rust protection and extended warranties.

This can be such a complex final chapter that we've written an entire section on it. Chapter 8 covers everything that might happen to you in the "business manager's" office.

When all the negotiating is done between you and the sales staff, you will be handed off to the business manager, as he's often called, to complete the paperwork. No matter what you told the original sales staff, you will be subjected, again, to a variety of sales pitches to entice you into buying financing or leasing packages, extended warranties, fabric-, paint-, and rust-protection services, alarm systems, and a whole hoopla of other products.

QUICK TIPS

NEGOTIATING ON USED CARS

If you're looking to negotiate a low price on a used car, try this strategy:

Inspect the car, and with a notepad and pencil keep a record of every blemish, scratch, or stone chip. Make a point of visibly noticing each imperfection, tracing the outline of a small dent with your fin-
gertips and softly clucking your tongue and shaking your head. Do this in front of the seller when possible.

If done properly, the strategy has the effect of making the seller feel less confident about their asking price for the car. Even professionals can fall for this trick when it's well executed. Refer to your list
regularly when the two of you are discussing the price of the car, and automatically deduct at least $50 to $100 from their asking price for every entry on the list. Use this strategy to help defend your offer and close the sale.

7

Leasing

IN THIS CHAPTER:

THE POPULARITY OF LEASING. Leasing a car has become one of the most popular ways of acquiring a new or used vehicle in North America. This section looks at the reasons why leasing has seen such a large increase in popularity among consumers.

THE LEASING SELF-TEST. Leasing is popular, but it's not for everyone. This self-test helps you determine whether or not a lease is right for you.

THE LEASING CONTRACT. Changes are happening across Canada regarding standard lease contracts. New regulations at the provincial level may soon become a nation-wide leasing standard.

LEARNING THE LANGUAGE. Leasing introduces some new terms that can be hard to understand and confusing to keep straight. This glossary of terms covers everything from closed-end policies to residual values.

READING THE ADS. Dealers and manufacturers like leasing, and most ads will emphasize this. Learning how to read them will save you time and frustration when you visit the dealer.

VISITING THE DEALER. This section provides some tips for consumers who are planning to lease their next car from a dealership.

THE POPULARITY OF LEASING

The 1990s might well be called "the decade of the lease." Open any newspaper and you'll be hard pressed not to come across a leasing ad. TV commercials no longer tell you the price of the car you're seeing. They tell you the monthly payment. Every car dealer you visit will ask if you are planning on leasing your new car. Leases are now available even on used cars.

QUICK TIPS

USED-CAR LEASING

Leasing is now available on used cars. This allows you to acquire an older car (reducing your exposure to depreciation) while enjoying the benefit of lower monthly payments, when compared to financing the car over a similar term. Also, if the car ends up being a lemon, you don't own it. That saves you the hassle of trying to unload it later. The drawback is that the terms on used cars are shorter than for new cars, often only one or two years. As a result, your monthly payments may be fairly high. If the factory warranty has run out, see if you can buy an extended warranty to cover any problems that might arise during the lease period.

Leasing has become such a popular way to finance a car that the December, 1997 issue of *Consumer Reports* magazine states that 40 percent of all new cars sold in Canada are now leased. That's up 10 times from 1989.

Among upscale cars, the leasing impact is even greater: Over half of all cars priced over $23 000 Cdn. are now being leased. Clearly, Canadians see leasing as an attractive option.

Dealerships also report that a number of leases are written to business people who prefer not to tie up their funds in depreciating assets. These buyers also like the tax advantages of leasing, and the convenience of having a new car every few years.

Car dealerships like to lease cars. It's perhaps their favourite way of making a sale. That's because a leased vehicle is really just a rented vehicle, so dealerships know that they'll be seeing that car again one day. They know the exact date the lease terminates, so they know when you'll be coming back to trade it in. They have an opportunity to earn your repeat business. Plus, they expect the car will be in good condition. Most leasing agreements include clauses that impose penalties if there are too many kilometres on the vehicle, or if the car shows damage beyond normal wear and tear when it comes back.

This explains why dealerships are so anxious to have you lease from them—it means a good shot at a sale at a specific point in the future. Not only do they get the profit from your lease, they can sell your leased car when it's turned in, and get a good crack at putting you into a new one! That's three sales opportunities. No wonder leasing ads dominate the automotive sections of newspapers.

So is this a route you should consider? Maybe.

The debate about whether to finance or lease has been raging for over a decade. Different sources offer conflicting theories on which course is better, and attempt to prove their positions with complex tables and calculations.

No one can agree on this issue. The April, 1995 issue of *Consumer Reports* magazine contains an article entitled "Lease instead of buy?" with a table that appears to prove that leasing is more expensive than conventional financing by up to five percent over four years.

That seems credible. But then car-buying guru James Bragg includes calculations in his best-selling book, *In the Driver's Seat* (New York: Random House, 1993), that show how leasing can save you eight percent of your car's total value over a three-year

QUICK TIPS

THE WISE LEASING STRATEGY

If you're on the fence between leasing and financing, and can't decide which avenue to take, consider this approach. Take the lease, but set aside the monthly equivalent of the financing payment and invest the difference. For example, if the difference between the lease payment and the finance cost is $100 a month, set that money aside for investment purposes, maybe as a pre-authorized deposit into a mutual fund. You'll be able to take advantage of a great investment tool known as dollar cost averaging, and you'll be building your personal wealth.

period when compared with conventional financing. Plus, the lease gives you additional cash flow, money that can be invested or simply spent.

THE LEASING SELF-TEST

Who's right? The simple answer is they both are—within the parameters they've set. Whether or not you should lease your next car is a complicated question that goes well beyond the amount of the monthly payment. Much depends on your personal financial situation and your priorities.

So where do you begin? Start by asking yourself whether a lease is right for you. Here's a self-test to help you answer that one. Answer each question with a simple yes or no.

Is Leasing Right For You?

- Do you want to drive a new car every few years?

- Do you drive fewer than 20 000 to 25 000 km a year per car?

- Do you want to drive a more expensive car than fits your monthly budget?

- Do you want to avoid a sizeable down payment on your new car?

- Are you willing to make monthly payments on a car indefinitely?

- Will your business make the payments for you?

Give yourself one point for each "yes" answer, zero for a "no." If your score is four or more, leasing is an option you should consider. If your score is three or less, try the next set of questions.

- Do you anxiously await "Car Payment Freedom Day," when the outstanding balance is paid off and you finally own your car outright?

- Do you keep your cars longer than five years?

- Do you drive more than 26 000 km per car each year?

- Can you handle a down payment of 20 percent or more on your new car?

- Can you purchase the new car outright?

Score this set the same way. If your total is three or more, forget leasing and look for a way to buy the car, keeping financing charges to a minimum. Of course, paying cash is always a better choice than either financing or leasing. You won't be caught in the interest-rate cycle, and you'll enjoy the freedom from monthly payments. However, 90 percent of consumers don't have the ready cash to buy outright.

A good lease contract will provide you with these benefits.

- You get a new car every few years, without having to worry about disposing of the old one.

- Your monthly payments will be less than if you bought the car using conventional financing. That allows you to obtain a more luxurious car than you could normally afford, or, if you prefer, to apply the difference to lower the monthly payment.

- You won't own a depreciating asset (although you will be paying the depreciation costs for the portion of the car you are using.).

- You won't need to find the cash for a down payment. No down payment is *required* on a lease. You can make a "capital cost reduction" payment if you choose—a payment to reduce the outstanding value of the lease, therefore lowering your monthly charge. Otherwise, pay the first and last month's "rent" plus applicable taxes and you can drive away in a brand-new car. (Note: Even though there are technically no such things as down payments on a lease, dealers often refer to capital cost reductions as down payments. They seem to think this practice avoids confusion. It doesn't. The concepts are quite different.)

- If this is an employer-supplied car, leasing can reduce the amount of taxable benefit that will be assessed. That's because Revenue Canada's formula for calculating the taxable benefit on a leased car is different from that applied to a car that's purchased outright.

THE LEASING CONTRACT

If you decide to lease, keep in mind you're not buying the car. You'll never own a leased car, unless you choose to buy it at the end of the agreement—which you can do only if the contract permits.

Leasing a car is rather like renting an apartment. You get the use of the car for the term of the contract. During that time, you make monthly payments, like rent, to the leasing company. But, even though it's the car you drive, it's not *your* car.

At the end of the term, you have to return the car to the leasing company. Terms can run from one year to five years, and the contract may contain a number of conditions. For example, some contracts allow you to purchase the car from the leasing company at an agreed-upon price. Others don't give you that choice—you have to let the leasing company take possession of "your" car. There can be clauses that assess penalty charges if mileage exceeds a stated limit over the term. You can also be hit with charges if the condition of the vehicle isn't satisfactory to the lessor (the leasing company). Finally, leasing a new vehicle exposes you to high depreciation costs, because you're driving the car during the years when it loses the largest percentage of its resale value.

LEARNING THE LANGUAGE

If you decide in favour of leasing, you'll have to learn some terminology. Understanding what the salesperson is saying may save you thousands of dollars. Here are some essential terms.

CLOSED-END LEASE

This type of lease sets a limit on the number of kilometres the car can be driven over the life of the lease and provides for a surcharge if this amount is exceeded. Under normal circumstances, you will not have an option to purchase the car when the lease ends. Maintenance is your responsibility. The vehicle must be returned in good condition, other than reasonable wear and tear. (When you bring it back, the car will be carefully scrutinized. If there's any body damage, mechanical problems, or upholstery rips, tears and burns, they'll be fixed at your expense.)

OPEN-END LEASE

This type of lease gives you more flexibility in the terms of the agreement, but might cost you more. It carries a fixed-lease rate for the duration of the lease that includes unlimited mileage. When the lease ends, you have two options.

You can buy the car for a preset amount (residual value).

You can return the car to the dealership for them to sell. In most cases, you will be on the hook for the difference if the car sells for less than the residual value. But you'll be credited with any money that's received in excess of the residual value. Ask for documentation or copies of the tenders, in writing, for evidence of the offered prices and who the tendering quotes were received from. People or companies bidding on the car should be independent of the leasing company.

CAPITALIZED COST

This is the purchase price agreed upon between you and your sales representative, plus any other costs you might have rolled into the lease contract (e.g., registration fees, sales taxes, extended warranties). If you've negotiated a price of $1000 off the MSRP, but your lease contract shows a capitalized cost that doesn't reflect that, raise a bit of hell.

CAPITAL COST REDUCTION

This is a payment made from you to the leasing company to reduce the capitalized cost of the vehicle. This is not a down payment, as no down payment is required to lease a car. This is a way of reducing the outstanding principal, so as to lower your monthly payments.

RESIDUAL VALUE

This is the estimated value of your car at the expiration of the lease contract. Think of it as a guaranteed resale value for your car. This amount is not included in the payments you'll be making over the period of the lease; it is the amount you have to pay at the end of the contract if you have the choice to buy the car.

Residual values aren't carved in stone. Typically, the residual, or "buyout," is set after taking into consideration the length of the term and the current resale values for similar cars. Because this amount is subtracted from the total being financed, many people believe they should negotiate as high a residual value as possible. The drawback to that approach is that it makes the vehicle harder to sell when the lease expires, because its "buyback" is higher than its street value. If you intend to buy the car at the end of the lease, this means you'll pay more than it's actually worth at that time. If you don't want to buy it but are guaranteeing the residual value to the leasing company, you may have to come up with an end payment of several hundred dollars. That's because the car won't command the price needed to match the residual value.

On the other hand, be careful of salespeople who offer what seems like too low a residual value. The first priority to car salespeople is profit. With a low residual value, they will make a higher profit on the vehicle when the lease expires and you turn in the keys. In the meantime, you're making higher monthly payments.

Residual value is a fine balance between how much the lessor wants for the car down the road and what you want to pay for the car over the term of the lease. Before you begin negotiating on this point, ask yourself what is

QUICK TIPS

BUYBACK OPTION SCHEDULE

Get a buyback schedule as part of the lease agreement. This will allow you to buy the car at any time during the lease period, at the price indicated on the schedule. Typically, a schedule will show a purchase price at six-month intervals, right up to the time the lease expires.

likely to happen to the car when the lease is up. Some people buy the car at that time as standard procedure. Others move on. Your answer will help determine your appropriate strategy for negotiating residual value.

READING THE ADS

The key to successful leasing is advance preparation. Start by looking through your weekend newspaper for special leasing deals. Be sure to read the fine print of any that catch your eye. The big bold numbers that say "$99 a month!" don't mean much if the fine print says you need to put up $20 000 in advance.

Here's an example from the Wheels section of *The Toronto Star*, Saturday November 8, 1997. It reads: "The '98 Neon. Big on room. And now bigger than ever on value. Lease it $299/month for 30 months. $0 down security deposit. Freight and taxes included. Own it $14,888 plus financing at 5.9% up to 60 months."

The ad goes on to list the features of the 1998 Neon. To the reader, the ad looks like a good deal. The numbers are printed in large bold print, and owning a car for only $299 a month, no money down, certainly seems like a good deal.

If you were to lease this car without reading the fine print first, you would be surprised at what happens two years down the road.

The fine print is the small type at the bottom of the ad. It tells you that during the 30 months of this lease, you'll pay out about $9000 to drive this car. You've got 51 000 kilometres, no more. If you go over that limit, you'll be charged nine cents a kilometre. The fine print also tells you that this is a closed-end lease, which means that you don't get to keep the car unless you negotiate that into the agreement. If you don't arrange this *before* you buy the car, there's nothing you can do when they take it away 30 months later. The ad does go on to inform you that there is no buyback *requirement*, but isn't quite as good at pointing out that there's also no buyback at all unless you bring it up. The fine print continues with information that the lease includes the freight and the taxes. It's nice to see a price that you don't have to add taxes to, isn't it? Everything else is your responsibility—the licensing, insurance, and registration.

This lease is for 30 months, which is good for the dealer: Three-year-old cars usually sell faster, and at a better price, than older models. These cars will be back in the dealer's inventory in time for the lucrative spring sales events in the year 2000, and with time to spare before they turn three years old. There's still plenty of warranty left on the vehicle, and with less than 51 000 km on the clock, they'll attract a good price.

This lease term may not be quite as attractive for individuals. The first two years of the car's life are the years in which it experiences its highest rates of depreciation. Longer-term leases tend to amortize those depreciation years.

Finally, the fine print tells you that this deal is negotiable. The line "Individual dealers may sell for less" is almost an invitation to ask for a better deal, and you should certainly do so. It's also required by law. Price fixing (a term applied to anyone who tries to set a fixed price for a specific product within a specific area) is illegal. (That's why you can actually negotiate on Saturn cars, the ones that have the special "one price," no dicker sticker!) The fact that this is negotiable is important knowledge, because this deal can (and should) be improved by the consumer.

First of all, never lease a car without ensuring that you have an option to purchase it. It is possible to negotiate a closed-end lease with an option to purchase the car at the end. This should be one of your first requests. Stay away from open-end leases, because they require the consumer to guarantee the end value of the car. A closed-end lease places that responsibility with the dealer, so that you can either take it or leave it 30 months down the road, without any hassles.

Second, you should negotiate a better price; $299 a month seems reasonable, but this deal can be made sweeter. Once you've opened the door to negotiating a deal, you may as well cover as many issues as possible. While negotiating the buyback option on this car, also try your luck at negotiating the monthly payment, the buyback amount, and even the kilometre restriction. Don't expect success in all areas when you negotiate, but do expect a few concessions.

And pore over the ads. As you become more familiar with the leasing lingo, you'll begin to see how the different factors of a lease deal are all linked together. Just remember to keep one eye on the fine print and to ask hard questions.

VISITING THE DEALER

When the time comes to visit the dealership, don't let the sales staff know that you plan to lease. Go through the negotiations to reach a final price as if you were going to buy the car outright. Then, when the process is complete, ask the salesperson for a lease price based on that figure.

He or she won't be pleased. Salespeople are trained to determine up front if the buyer is going to lease, finance, or pay cash. That way, figures can be discussed in the appropriate mode. Sales staff prefer to negotiate in terms of monthly payments. The numbers are smaller, and it's easier to convince you to pay an extra $20 a month on a contract than to ask you to pay an extra $1000 on the list price. (In fact, $20 a month over 48 months is equal to an extra $1000 on the total purchase price of the vehicle!)

So you'll be asked several times if you plan to lease the car. Simply respond that you haven't decided yet, and keep the negotiations focused on the complete price of the vehicle, not the monthly payments.

When you finally do ask for lease figures based on the agreed-upon price, make sure you find out the lease factor (or interest rate) and the residual value of the contract. Also determine what kind of contract it is, a closed- or open-end agreement. Finally, take all the information home with you, along with a copy of the contract, and read it over carefully. Calculate the monthly payments with the interest rate and the residual

LEASING 81

value and the term to make sure they equal the agreed-upon price. Read over the clauses for penalty charges or conditions. If you disagree with anything, negotiate.

If the dealership won't allow you to do this (some are notoriously reluctant to let you out the door with an unsigned contract), go someplace else. There's always someone else who will be happy to sell you a car.

QUICK TIPS

THE LEASING BUYBACK

If we can leave you with one important leasing tip that will serve you well, it's this: Always insist upon an "optional" buyback price upon termination of your lease contract. This optional buyback gives you the flexibility to purchase your leased car rather than pay excessive mileage charges at lease end. This strategy also allows you the opportunity to sell your leased car yourself. Make sure that the buyback price is optional, so that you can take it or leave it.

8

Warranties

IN THIS CHAPTER:

WHAT'S IN A WARRANTY? The major components of a standard warranty are explained. Knowing exactly how to read the warranty of the vehicle you're buying tells you what your rights are in the months and years to come.

EXTENDED WARRANTIES. Sometimes they're good deals, but sometimes buy-

ing an extended warranty is just throwing away money. A lot depends on your personal situation, as covered in this section.

SHOPPING TIPS. Some points to consider when purchasing an extended warranty for your new or used car.

WHAT'S IN A WARRANTY?

Every new car sold in Canada comes equipped with an extremely important feature, one you won't see when you turn your key in the ignition. The most valuable component of your new-car purchase is its warranty. The manufacturer of your new car guarantees that the vehicle has been built to a level of quality that will keep it in good operating condition for a specified length of time. It is your insurance policy, securing your peace of mind that you have not bought a lemon.

Warranties differ among manufacturers. You'll find warranties that cover different components of a car for different lengths of time. The best warranties in Canada are offered by the luxury manufacturers of Lexus and Infiniti, but you may find a warranty that suits your specific needs with a different company. Many warranties have kilometre restrictions, which may not interest drivers who accumulate a lot of highway kilometres driving across Canada or to the United States.

Some drivers find that they can't fit a basic warranty with their driving habits. At an extra cost, extended warranties can be purchased that improve the basic warranty offered by the manufacturer. Whether you should purchase an extended warranty depends primarily on what basic warranty is already provided and your long-term plans for your car.

Extended warranties are also popular among used-car buyers who are purchasing a car with little or no warranty left. Some dealerships offer free extended warranties on their used cars as an incentive to attract buyers.

Whether you're buying a new or used car, the warranty that is offered with the vehicle is something you should consider very carefully.

Your first step is to read carefully the basic warranty that comes with the car you've chosen. Your sales representative will guide you through the details, but most warranties follow a similar pattern. If you're buying your car from a private seller, consult the owner's manual of the vehicle for specific warranty information. If you can't locate the owner's manual, you can purchase one from most dealership service departments (you can also ask for a photocopy of the warranty section of the guide if you want to save about $20).

Standard warranties are composed of four elements: the power train (or major mechanical components) warranty, the complete vehicle (or bumper-to-bumper) warranty, the rust perforation warranty, and the pollution-control warranty.

Major mechanical components include the engine, the wheel axles, suspension, steering, brakes, and electronic parts. These elements are usually covered under warranty for five years or 100 000 kilometres, whichever comes first.

Bumper-to-bumper warranties cover the entire car. Windows, door latches, trunk releases: anything in or on the body of the car is warrantied against defects in material or workmanship, usually for a minimum of three years or 60 000 kilometres, whichever comes first.

Pollution-control warranties cover the exhaust system and guarantee the vehicle will adhere to national emission control regulations for at least five years or 80 000 kilometres, whichever comes first.

Rust perforation warranties are usually set at five years, unlimited kilometres. They insure the body of your car against rust that eats through the metal from the inside out. Note: These warranties will *not* protect you against surface rust, or rust that is caused from paint chips or dents.

Although these four components are found in most basic warranties, the period of coverage may differ. For instance, Chrysler vehicles include a major components warranty that runs for three years or 60 000 kilometres with a limited roadside assistance warranty.

In essence, these are not really warranties, but insurance contracts. The manufacturer is insuring parts of the car against breakdown or failure during the term of the "policy." Whether you should purchase additional insurance is a question you can answer only after considering your driving habits, the length of time you'll have the car, and its reliability record.

QUICK TIPS

TRANSFERRING WARRANTIES

In many cases, a warranty is non-transferable, so if you sell the car to someone else, they can't use it. If you decide to buy an extended warranty, see if it can be made transferable, at least to one owner. Having that extra protection will enhance the appeal and resale value of the car.

QUICK TIPS

EXTENDED WARRANTIES

If you're leasing a car with the intention of keeping it only three or four years, buying an extended warranty doesn't make sense. The basic warranty covers you. If, however, you're buying a car with the intention of keeping it until it falls apart, an extended warranty is worth considering.

EXTENDED WARRANTIES

You'll most likely be offered several different extended warranty packages. Most convert the standard warranty to six years or longer. So, if the standard warranty includes three-year bumper-to-bumper protection, the same coverage will be extended for the additional term.

What will differ will be the kilometre restrictions. Some will offer only 120 000 kilometres of coverage. Others will protect the car up to 180 000 kilometres. If you can afford it, you can purchase unlimited kilometre warranties.

Are extended warranties a good deal? In many cases, no. You have to compare the cost of the warranty against any problems that might arise from manufacturer defect down the road. Warranties do not protect you against normal wear and tear, which is what you're more likely to encounter after four or five years of ownership.

Suppose you buy the extended warranty and something goes wrong after a few years. If there's a dispute, you may have to prove the problem occurred because of a manufacturer's defect, not because of wear and tear or abuse. This is not always easy.

Canadian driving conditions are among the worst in the world. Temperatures can reach the mid-30s during summer, and drop as low as −30 or worse during the winter, depending on where you live. Our roads are covered with salt for half the year, and under repair the other half. Potholes appear during spring. So wear and tear is anything but "normal" in our climate.

In addition, many extended warranties include deductibles, often as high as $250. If the repair job costs less than the deductible, you pay. The warranty contributes nothing. Some don't supply overnight service warranty cars (loaners).

A basic extended warranty will cost about $900 (maximum $1800). That might not seem like much if it's rolled into your monthly payment, but as a repair cost it's expensive. That money will pay for a complete brake job, or a rebuilt exhaust system, or work to most of the major components on your car.

QUICK TIPS

WARRANTY SECURITY

Find out who will be responsible for fulfilling the terms of the warranty and whether it can be sold off. There have been cases where warranties have turned out to be invalid because the company ultimately responsible for the servicing went belly-up. The best warranty is one that is guaranteed by the manufacturer.

SHOPPING TIPS

So are there any circumstances under which you should buy an extended warranty?

Yes, there are. If the car is a demonstrator with several thousand kilometres already on it, an extended warranty might be a good purchase to protect you against poor treatment of the car during the break-in period, before you decided to buy it.

An extended warranty might also be considered if you frequently drive long distances, and are facing a scenario whereby the kilometres on the car might void the standard warranty several years before its normal termination date.

You may also wish to refer to the car's reliability record, which you'll find in such publications as *Consumer Reports*. If the make has a reputation for requiring frequent repairs, an extended warranty may be worth the investment.

Extended warranties are a sweetener for the dealership and the salesperson who sells them to you. The profit is shared amongst the issuing company, the dealer, and the sales representative, so everyone will do their best to convince you it's a good deal. Don't be pressured; act in your own best interest.

QUICK TIPS

WARRANTY ALTERNATIVES

As an alternative to buying a warranty, put $800 (or whatever the dealership quotes as their price) into a money market mutual fund for a few years, as your own personal insurance policy. If you never have any major repair bills, you'll be richer by $800 plus the interest you've earned over that time.

9

The Extras

IN THIS CHAPTER:

PADDING THE DEAL. Should you buy those extras at a dealership?

RUST PROTECTION. Rust proofing is an old and simple industry. The application of a super-concentrated layer of rust protection to a car's body (inside and out) makes the car much more resistant to rust, resulting in a longer life for the car's body. There are three different types of rust protection, and widely varying prices. This section explains how to buy rust protection for your automobile without paying through the nose.

PAINT SEALANT AND FABRIC PROTECTION.
Like rust protection, paint sealant and fabric protector are sold by dealers to lengthen the life and beauty of your car's body. Unlike rust protection, these are a very poor deal. This section explains how to purchase these services at up to a 90 percent discount from dealer prices.

OTHER EXTRAS. Dealers offer many extras, like life insurance and alarm systems. In large communities (like Toronto or Vancouver), auto theft has become a rising concern among vehicle owners. This section looks at the value of alarm systems.

It also considers a variety of cosmetic extras that can be purchased for a car or truck, like tinted windows or decals.

PADDING THE DEAL

Dealers will try to get you to purchase extras with your car. Once the sale of the vehicle has been negotiated, most salespeople will try to pad the deal with additional expenses. Some of these extras are worthwhile investments, while others are simply thinly veiled grabs for your pocketbook.

Depending on the dealer, you'll be offered these extras either by the salesperson or sometimes by a new face called "the business manager" or "the finance and insurance specialist." No matter who tries to sell you these products, you'll likely experience just as much price resistance and negotiating pressure as you did with your car purchase.

Protection deals usually come in three parts. They can be bought individually, or as a package for a small discount. Of the three, rust proofing is the biggest seller, although fabric protection and paint sealant also attract lots of dollars.

We recommend that, under most circumstances, these services not be bought through a dealership. Here's why.

RUST PROTECTION

Rust proofing comes in several different forms. You can buy it in an oil-based application, a wax-based one, or as a tar- and asphalt-based system. These formats have been around for several years, and you'll hear good and bad things about each, depending on whom you talk to.

The long and the short of it is that it doesn't matter much which kind of rust proofing you get. What matters is how well it's applied.

But before you even get to that point, ask yourself whether you should buy a rust-proofing package at all, either from the dealer or through an independent company.

In most parts of the country, we use a lot of salt on our roads in the winter to reduce the build-up of ice and snow. The salt melts the ice, leaving the roads clear, though wet and slushy.

Water is one of the main causes of rust. Rust forms as metal oxidizes, that is, as it's exposed to oxygen. There's oxygen in our air. There's oxygen in our water. Obviously, it's hard to keep metal from rusting.

Car manufacturers do a lot to help us out. Automobiles are usually dipped in a rust-proofing bath before they're painted. The body is often constructed from metal alloys that resist rust fairly well. And cars are painted with so many coats these days that they're pretty well protected from bare metal exposure to the elements.

But all of this becomes of little value once the paint chips, or a dent or scratch exposes the metal, or thin cracks in the doors or window ledges get filled with salt and water.

Salt will accelerate the rusting process. So once it combines with water and gets into your car's body, there's very little you can do.

Except, of course, to rust proof your car. That's why every Canadian who buys a new car should consider rust proofing it. That's true even if you live in one of the balmy coastal areas of British Columbia, where the problem is sea salt.

Even if you're going to resell your car within a few years, have it rust proofed anyway. Rust can destroy a car long before it naturally wears out. If you don't rust proof, you could end up with a vehicle that is still mechanically sound but unsightly, unsaleable, and, perhaps, not even roadworthy.

Rust proofing is a process whereby the metal surfaces of a car are coated with a protective film that prevents moisture and dirt from gaining a foothold. When applied properly, the rust proofing compound will protect both the inner and outer surfaces of the car, and seep into the deepest nooks and crevices of the body, which is where rust usually begins. For this reason, oil-based rust proofing is usually your best bet. It's thinner than tar and asphalt compounds, which means it will spread throughout the inner surfaces of the car more easily.

Obviously, for the rust-proofing job to be done properly, the solution has to be sprayed on the inside of the body—not an easy task once the car is built.

But a good garage will do the job properly. The door panels should be removed, so that the compound is sprayed directly onto the inner mechanisms. Window moldings should be pulled aside and the spray applied into the exposed cracks. Carpeting should be removed so that the spray can be applied to the car floor. As well, the car should be placed on a lift and raised several feet so that the underbody can be sprayed. It should be a long, painstaking job. And you should be prepared to pay a good dollar for it to be done right.

QUICK TIPS

DO YOU NEED TO RUST PROOF YOUR CAR?

The answer isn't a simple yes or no. Like leasing, rust protection is something that is of benefit to some and a waste of money to others. If you drive more than 30 000 kilometres a year, park your car exposed to the elements, and collect a lot of stone chips on your car from highway driving in rural areas, you may be a rust high-risk candidate. Given the extreme weather conditions experienced in Canada, every bit of protection helps, especially if you have long-term plans with your new car.

But don't pay big money for a poor job. Find out how your dealership applies their rust proofing. Contact independants for competitive quotes, and find out how their application procedures differ. Look in the Yellow Pages under Rust Proofing.

A good rust-proofing job should cost in the $400 to $500 range. The price quoted by your dealer may be quite a bit higher, perhaps $650. Don't hesitate to negotiate if you want them to do the job. There's a lot of profit built into a rust-proofing package, and you might be able to keep some of it for yourself.

Another key point: There is no single-application rust proofing we know of that's effective. For your car to be properly protected, the work needs to be re-done at regular intervals. An annual visit is best. Any rust-proofing deal you negotiate should be on that basis. If the dealer wants to charge you big dollars for a one-time service, say thanks a lot and go visit a Rust Check centre.

PAINT SEALANT AND FABRIC PROTECTION

These packages are also sold by the dealership. Each typically costs about $150 to $250. They aren't worth it.

Canadian Tire (or any other hardware store) sells a variety of car care products. In the automotive section you'll find a wide range of paint sealant waxes and fabric protection sprays, all priced in roughly the $10 to $20 range. It's pretty obvious what the better deal is.

These products come with detailed application instructions, most of which simply require about three hours of free time and a little elbow grease. Most people don't even consider it work, as it's a good way to "bond" with your new car, giving you a good opportunity to inspect the vehicle thoroughly for any problems you may have missed.

There are also numerous secondary stores that will apply these products for you for a nominal labour charge. Consult with auto detailing and custom cleaning facilities for more information. And keep an eye out for young entrepreneurs looking to make some cash between school terms—custom car servicing is a popular university part-time job and a source of some great value prices.

OTHER EXTRAS

Dealerships offer many other extras that they might try to tempt you with. Here's a quick run-down.

LIFE INSURANCE

The sales pitch is that your car loan will be paid off should you or your spouse pass away before the end of the financing term. What's the point? Typical payouts on a life insurance policy will cover any outstanding car loan, with money to spare. Check with your life insurance company first.

ALARM SYSTEMS

A car alarm! The bane of suburban shopping malls! Do you need one of these fancy toys? If you think you do, shop around. Dealerships usually inflate their prices. And their labour charges are likely to be higher, as well.

There are numerous alarm and anti-theft systems available for today's automobiles. Prices run the gamut from $30 to $3000. At the affordable end of the spectrum you'll find devices like "The Club," which can be purchased at most department stores. This product locks your steering wheel into place, preventing thieves from turning the wheels and driving away. For its price it's good protection, but it won't deter professional car thieves who use tow trucks and advanced equipment to net their prey.

But better protection leads to higher prices. Sensitive electronic car alarms can detect when a car's door is being opened and immediately respond with noise and flashing lights. Alarms like this aren't cheap—usually around $500 to $1500. But, again, if a thief is determined he or she will most likely be able to de-activate the alarm within 30 seconds. What's more alarming is that most people simply ignore the honk-ing, flashing lights, and sirens of these protection systems. The rash of false alarms set off in our cities every day because of sensors being tuned too high has desensitized passersby, meaning a thief may in fact have several minutes in which to de-activate such a car alarm before attracting any real attention, as long as he or she is discreet.

At the most expensive end of the spectrum is a new type of car alarm that is much more interactive. Using Global Positioning Satellites (GPS) orbiting the earth, alarm companies are able to track subscriber vehicles in case of emergencies. These alarms also make use of the car's cellular phone to make direct voice contact with the driver of the car. Alarms like this range from $3000 to $5000.

TINTED WINDOWS

Tinting a car's windows can dramatically affect how the car looks, and will definitely affect your view from the interior of the car. When you have the windows tinted, a layer of tinted plastic is applied over the glass, reducing the amount of light that pass-es through it. Tinting a car's windows provides four advantages.

1. You will have increased privacy. It's harder to see inside, so you're safe to sing along with your favourite radio songs during rush hour, content in the knowl-edge that no-one can see you.

2. The cabin temperatures will be lower. With the windows tinted, it's easier to keep the interior of the car cool during hot days. Using the air conditioner less also results in better fuel mileage.

3. Many cars look better with a nice tint. With so many different types of tint, you can make almost any car look better. Luxury cars look good with a gold tint, while sports cars look more aggressive with the darkest tint possible.

4. Tinting does not cost a lot. If you're looking for an inexpensive way to touch up a vehicle and make it look unique, consider a tint. Some cars can be done for as little as $99.

Tinting your windows also has its disadvantages.

1. The biggest problem with tinting your windows is that it reduces your visi-bility. You should aim to preserve as much visibility as possible. Side windows should never be tinted as dark as the rear windows because it's harder to see cars beside you than it is to see the ones behind. The windshield should never be tinted.

2. If done poorly, a tinted window will develop "fingers," which are bubbles of air trapped between the glass and the plastic film. When you're shopping for a place to tint your windows, ask about guarantees and warranties against fingers and other bubbling or peeling.

3. Tints can be scratched from the inside. Because of this, it's probably a bad idea to tint the windows of a car that carries young children. Kids might have more fun drawing on the windows than in a colouring book, but those scratches are permanent. Be careful.

There is a less expensive way to personalize your vehicle that doesn't involve tinting. Many department stores and specialty auto detailing shops carry car stickers that can be applied to the body of your car. You can get stripes, splashes, flames, and names. They can be applied at home, in your garage, with warm water and a squeegee, but it's best to read the instructions and practise a bit. Once a decal is in position, it's hard to alter and hard to remove. As with any "modification" you make to your vehicle, think long and hard before going ahead.

10

The Bill of Sale

IN THIS CHAPTER:

SLOWING DOWN. It's vitally important that consumers not rush the final stage of a vehicle purchase—the signing of the bill of sale. After several hours of negotiating, it's necessary to switch gears and slow everything down to make sure you don't make a mistake. This section explains how to find the time to read the contract thoroughly.

BREAKING IT DOWN. A typical dealership bill of sale is a double-sided document that can be hard to read and harder to understand. This section includes step-by-step descriptions of all the relevant information from a typical bill of sale.

THE CLAUSES. This section describes what each clause means on a typical bill of sale, which ones to have removed, and which ones to add yourself.

PRIVATE SALES. The most important part of a private sales contract is pointed out.

SLOWING DOWN

Whether the car you buy is new or used, dealership sold or bought from a private seller, you'll encounter a bill of sale. Dealerships use sales forms that are complicated and full of clauses, while private sellers may be content to write you a receipt on an old piece of paper towel. In either case, you need to know what your rights are, and how to properly read and understand a bill of sale.

Everything said or promised up until now is not binding unless it is confirmed in writing on a bill of sale. You may have fought for hours for the price you want with the equipment you desire, but if you put your signature to a legal document that doesn't include everything you asked for, there's very little you can do to get out of it later.

So don't be in a rush to sign a bill of sale so you can get home to dinner. Take your time. Read it carefully. Make sure you fully understand everything in it. It doesn't matter if it's not neatly typed or computer processed. Even a handwritten bill of sale is legally binding if it includes your signature and the authorized signature of the seller.

QUICK TIPS

CLAUSES

Read all the clauses before you sign a bill of sale. You can add your own clauses and remove some dealership clauses. The sales bill you sign should reflect your needs, because you are the customer.

Don't read the sales contract while sitting at a desk with the salesperson. You want to read this document as carefully and slowly as you can, away from the pressures of the sales experience. Here are a few ways to find some time and some privacy to look over the contract.

Take a seat in the service waiting area of the dealership. There will be other people in there with you, but they'll all be waiting for their cars to be ready in the service department. Here you can sit comfortably for as long as you need to read the contract. You can also help yourself to coffee if it is available.

Ask to be given an executive office if one is free. Many dealerships have private offices for their senior staff, and there's usually one or two of them available because dealership staff often work in shifts. An office where you can close the door and shut out the sounds of the dealership is a great place to relax and read the bill of sale.

Leave the dealership completely. Take the bill of sale with you and spend some time at a local coffee shop or restaurant. Take the opportunity to relax, have something to eat or drink, and read through the contract at your leisure. If necessary, you can also take the contract home with you and go over it there.

No matter where you go to read the contract, you should ensure that you have an opportunity to take a break from the sales experience. Even if none of the above options is available to you, you can at least ask the salesperson to leave the desk/office/cubicle until you are ready to proceed.

This final step is usually the hardest part of the car-buying process. If you've just spent three hours dickering over prices and options, the last thing you want to do is sit and read a lot of small-print legalese in the presence of the sales staff.

BREAKING IT DOWN

Fortunately, most dealerships in Canada use a standard bill of sale, which doesn't differ much from province to province. That gives us the opportunity to explain in detail what you are likely to find in the sales contract when you purchase your car.

If you're buying your car from a private seller, you'll still want to ensure that there is a sales bill of some sort that changes hands. Refer to the end of this chapter for information on private sales contracts.

Figures 10.1 and 10.2 are reproductions of both sides of a standard dealer bill of sale. Side one is where information about you and your new car is written. Side two is mostly composed of legal clauses. Let's go through a typical bill of sale.

FIGURE 10.1   BILL OF SALE (FRONT)

[Dealer's name and address]

DATE

PURCHASER		HOME PHONE NO.	BUSINESS PHONE NO	OCCUPATION	
ADDRESS	APT. NO.	CITY		PROVINCE	POSTAL CODE
DRIVERS LIC. NO.	INSURANCE NO.	POLICY NO.	EXPIRY DATE	INS. AGENT	

I, THE PURCHASER, AGREE TO PURCHASE THE FOLLOWING VEHICLE FROM YOU, THE DEALER, ON THE TERMS SET OUT ON THE FRONT AND BACK OF THIS PAGE.

VEHICLE DESCRIPTION

☐ NEW ☐ USED	☐ POLICE VEHICLE ☐ TAXICAB	☐ DAILY RENTAL ☐ OTHER	YEAR	MAKE	MODEL	COLOUR	LIC. NO.
V.I.N				STOCK NO		SAFETY STANDARDS CERTIFICATE NO.	
IF MANUFACTURER WARRANTY APPLICABLE TIME IS MEASURED FROM		19	DISTANCE TRAVELLED	KM ☐ MI ☐	PURCHASER'S INITIAL		

BASIC VEHICLE AND OPTIONS

BASIC VEHICLE (MSRP)

OPTIONAL EXTRAS

TOTAL BASIC VEHICLE AND OPTIONAL EXTRAS PRICE ▶

TOTAL ▶

PRE-DELIVERY EXPENSE

TOTAL SALE PRICE ▶

PURCHASE PRICE AND PAYMENT

TOTAL SALE PRICE	▶	
FREIGHT		
FEDERAL AIR CONDITIONER TAX		
TAX FOR FUEL CONSUMPTION		
ADMINISTRATION FEE		139 00

PRODUCT NAME AND DESCRIPTION | WARRANTY PERIOD NO. OF MONTHS | NO. OF KMS | DATE OF COMMENCEMENT

TOTAL VEHICLE PRICE	▶	
TRADE-IN ALLOWANCE		
TOTAL VEHICLE PRICE LESS TRADE-IN ALLOWANCE		
PROVINCIAL SALES TAX ON TOTAL VEHICLE PRICE LESS TRADE-IN ALLOWANCE		
G.S.T. ON TOTAL VEHICLE PRICE ($)		
LICENSE FEE ☐ TRANSFER ☐ NEW PLATES		
FUEL (INCLUDES G.S.T.) ·		35 00
PAYOUT ON LIENS AGAINST TRADE-IN		
G.S.T. REGISTRANT NO. ( )		
FUEL TAX CONSERVATION REBATE		

TRADE-IN DESCRIPTION AND LIEN DISCLOSURE

☐ DAILY RENTAL ☐ TAXICAB	☐ POLICE VEHICLE	V.I.N.	
YEAR	MAKE		MODEL
COLOUR	G.S.T. REGISTRANT NO		G.S.T. ON TRADE IN $
DISTANCE TRAVELLED ☐ KM ☐ MI	LIEN HOLDER		AMT OF OUTSTANDING LIENS $
REMARKS			

INITIAL HERE   AMOUNT DUE ON DELIVERY CERTIFIED BY FUNDS ▶

TOTAL PURCHASE PRICE ▶

DEPOSIT ☐ CASH ☐ CHEQUE ☐ C. CARD

AMOUNT FINANCED (SUBJECT TO LENDER'S APPROVAL)

AMOUNT DUE ON DELIVERY ▶

FINANCING TERMS

PRINCIPAL AMOUNT	
LIFE INSURANCE (IF REQUESTED)	
ACCIDENT AND HEALTH INSURANCE (IF REQUESTED)	
LOSS OF INCOME INSURANCE (IF REQUESTED)	
P.S.T. ON TOTAL INSURANCE	
REGISTRATION FEE	
TOTAL TO BE FINANCED (SUBJECT TO LENDER'S APPROVAL)	
COST OF BORROWING %	
AMOUNT OF PAYMENTS $	NO OF PAYMENTS	PAYMENTS START DATE

ACCEPTANCE OF TERMS

I HAVE READ THE TERMS ON THE FRONT AND BACK OF THIS PAGE AND AGREE THAT YOU HAVE NOT MADE ANY PROMISES TO ME, NOR ARE THERE ANY OTHER TERMS RELATING TO THIS AGREEMENT, EXCEPT AS WRITTEN ON THE FRONT AND BACK OF THIS PAGE AND THAT THIS AGREEMENT WILL ONLY BE EFFECTIVE WHEN SIGNED BY YOUR AUTHORIZED REPRESENTATIVE.

X_____   X_____
PURCHASER'S SIGNATURE   CO-SIGNER (IF ANY)

NAME AND POSITION OF AUTHORIZED REPRESENTATIVE

SIGNATURE OF AUTHORIZED REPRESENTATIVE   REG. NO
X

SALESPERSON'S NAME

SALESPERSON'S SIGNATURE   REG. NO

FIGURE 10.2   BILL OF SALE (BACK)

1.   **Distance Travelled.**   You represent to me that to the best of your knowledge the distance travelled by the Vehicle is as shown on the other side of this page and, in the case of a Trade-In, I represent to you that to the best of my knowledge the distance travelled by the Trade In is as shown on the other side of this page.

2.   **Original Pollution Equipment.**   You will ensure, in the case of a used Vehicle, and I will ensure, in the case of a Trade-In, that all original pollution control equipment on the vehicle certified under the Motor Vehicle Safety Act of Canada is intact and operational at the time of delivery.

3.   **Safety Standards Certificate and Transfer Documents.**   I acknowledge that the motor vehicle permit for the Vehicle cannot be transferred to me unless I obtain a Safety Standards Certificate. If I do not request a Safety Standards Certificate you will deliver the Vehicle to me with an Unfit Motor Vehicle Permit and I will be responsible, at my sole cost, for removing the Vehicle from your premises. I authorize you on my behalf to make all applications and obtain all permits required to transfer the Vehicle in accordance with this Agreement.

4.   **Trade-Ins.**   I will transfer the Trade-In to you at the time that you deliver the Vehicle to me, or at such earlier time as we may agree to, free and clear of all liens (other than the liens which I have disclosed to you on the other side of this page). At the time of transfer, the Trade-In will be equipped and in the same condition, except for reasonable wear and tear, as it is on the date of this Agreement. If the Trade-In is not in the same condition, I may pay you for all necessary repairs or agree to reduce the Trade-In Allowance by the cost of the repairs. If we are unable to make arrangements which are satisfactory to both of us for the payment of any necessary repairs, this Agreement will be cancelled and you will be entitled to deduct your damages from my Deposit. If I transfer the Trade-In to you prior to the Vehicle being delivered to me, the Trade-In will form part of my Deposit

5.   **Manufacturer's Suggested Retail Price.**   If the Vehicle is new the Basic Vehicle Price and the prices of the Optional Extras are the manufacturer's suggested retail prices. If the Vehicle is being ordered by you from the manufacturer and there is any increase in the manufacturer's suggested retail prices after the date of this Agreement, the increases will be added to the Total Basic Vehicle and Optional Extras Price. If I refuse to pay the increase in the Amount Due on Delivery, you will have the right to waive the increase or to cancel this Agreement and return my Deposit.

6.   **Payment of Additional and Increased Taxes.**   If any federal or provincial taxes relating to the Vehicle or my purchase of the Vehicle under this Agreement are increased after the date of this Agreement and prior to the taking delivery of the Vehicle, I will pay you the amount of the increased taxes at the time of delivery.

7.   **Financing Information.**   If financing is to be provided to me, you represent to me that you have complied with Section 24 of the Consumer Protection Act of Ontario.

8.   **Ownership Transfers Only Upon Payment in Full.**   I agree that I will not become the owner of the Vehicle or have any other interest whatsoever in the Vehicle until I have paid the Amount Due on Delivery in full (including the amount of any increases resulting from increased taxes or changes in the manufacturer's suggested retail prices). I will pay you by certified cheque unless we otherwise agree.

9.   **Delays in the Delivery of the Vehicle.**   If the Vehicle is to be ordered from the manufacturer and you are unable to deliver the Vehicle to me within 90 days of the date of this Agreement, you will notify me in writing of the reason for the delay and thereafter either one of us may cancel this Agreement by giving written notice of the cancellation to the other person. Unless we agree in writing to a new delivery date, this Agreement will be cancelled automatically at the end of the 5 day period following my receipt of your notice of the delay. If you are unable to deliver the Vehicle to me by the new delivery date, this Agreement will be cancelled automatically. If this Agreement is cancelled for any of the above reasons, you will return my Deposit and neither one of us will have any further obligations under this Agreement.

10.   **Failure to Accept Delivery or to Pay.**   If I fail to accept delivery of the Vehicle within 7 days of you notifying me by registered mail that the Vehicle is available for delivery, or if I fail to pay you the full Amount Due on Delivery, you will be entitled, in addition to any other rights or remedies you may have, to cancel this Agreement and to deduct the amount of your damages from my Deposit.

11.   **Explanation of Damages.**   If you keep any part of my Deposit you will provide me with a written calculation and brief explanation of your damages.

12.   **Dealing with Trade-Ins as Deposits.**   If my Deposit includes a Trade-In, you may sell it and upon the completion of the sale my Deposit will be increased by the amount of the Trade-In Allowance, less any amounts paid by you to reduce any outstanding liens. If I am entitled to the return of my Deposit and you have not sold the Trade-In, you will transfer the Trade-In back to me and I will pay you for the Safety Standards Certificate and all other costs associated with transferring the Trade-In back into my name, all repairs and improvements which you may have made to the Trade-In and for all payments which you may have made to reduce any outstanding liens.

We'll start at the top of Figure 10.1, the first page of the contract. The document must legally define the parties in the transaction, which is why your name, address, and phone number are required.

Keep in mind as you go through the contract that any mistakes will provide you with an avenue of appeal if the deal turns sour down the road. Pay close attention to what information is being recorded, and where.

1. **Dealer's name and address.** This legally establishes who the seller is.

2. **Date of sale.** Make sure this is filled in with the date that you sign the contract. You might be required to sign two bills of sale, the first on the day you agree to purchase the car, the second on the day that you pick it up and the money changes hands. Make sure that the date is correct on any contracts you sign.

3. **Your name and address.** This legally defines the purchaser.

4. **New or used.** If you are purchasing a new car, make sure this is indicated in this box. Demos qualify as new cars. Also, notice the line just above this area, which reads "I, the purchaser, agree to purchase the following vehicle from you, the dealer, on the terms set out on the front and back of this page." This is the most important part of the document, because it is the legal declaration of your intent to purchase.

5. **Vehicle description.** This section deals with a legal description of the vehicle you are buying. Make sure that all the information is correct. Some of these specifics may not appear on bills of sale in certain provinces: year, make, model name, model number, colour, trim, top colour, serial number (VIN), dealer's stock number, odometer reading (if new, should say new, if used, number of kilometres at date of sale), purchaser's initials—you will be asked to initial this box to confirm the information about the car you are buying.

6. **Optional equipment.** On the left side of the page is a description of the optional equipment specified for this vehicle. The small print at the top explains that, if the vehicle is a new one, options are to be listed with prices that reflect the manufacturer's suggested retail price (MSRP). The information set out in this section will include the full list price for the car and the options you've chosen, not the prices you've negotiated.

7. **Total basic vehicle.** This is the sum of the basic vehicle list price plus the options or option packages you've chosen. The line following is deliberately left blank, but if it were titled it would say "Manager's allowance" or "Special discount." This is where the sum total of your hours of negotiating will be calculated.

8. **Total.** This is where the actual purchase price of the car is listed, before freight, taxes, and all the rest of the extras.

9. **Pre-delivery expense.** This is a charge levied by the dealership to prepare

the car for pick-up. When dealers receive vehicles from the factory, they are covered inside and out with cardboard, pieces of plastic, and other forms of protection to keep them from being damaged during shipping. They may also sit on the lot for several days to several months before being sold, and can get pretty dirty. The pre-delivery expense is a charge to clean up the car, remove any shipping protectors, and wax it. The charge can run anywhere from nothing to several hundred dollars.

You can sometimes get a dealer to waive this cost. There's no harm in trying. If he won't waive it, at least ensure that you aren't paying too much. A good pre-delivery inspection will take about two hours. Compare the charge against the dealership's hourly labour rate, and make sure it matches up. A reasonable target price is anywhere between $90 and $150.

10. Total sale price. This amount is added to the previous total to arrive at an all-inclusive sale price, which is shown at the bottom left of the page. This is carried over to the first line of the "Purchase Price and Payment" list on the right side of the page. Make sure these numbers match up.

The following section deals with any extra charges to be added to the purchase price of the car. These may include:

11. Freight. This is an amortized cost of shipping vehicles to dealers anywhere in the country. Instead of charging people in Alliston, Ontario virtually nothing for delivering a Honda Civic that was built there, while people in Vancouver pay huge costs for shipping the same car across the country, a standard charge is levied against everyone. It differs from one manufacturer to the next, depending on where the cars are built. It is non-negotiable.

12. Federal air conditioner tax. Currently $100. If you aren't getting air conditioning, you don't pay this tax. Otherwise, you do. Like all taxes, it's non-negotiable.

13. Provincial tire tax. This differs among provinces, and not all provinces charge it. The tax is imposed on each tire the car comes with, including the spare. There's no way out of it, unless you plan to drive on the rims.

14. Tax for fuel consumption. This tax depends on the gas mileage rating of your new vehicle. Some cars, like the 1998 Dodge Neon with standard transmission, are so fuel efficient that they get a tax credit, which is shown on the bill of sale. Others, notably trucks, aren't as lucky. This tax can run to several thousand dollars. To avoid an unpleasant surprise at this stage, ask what the cost will be while you're negotiating the price of the car.

15. Administration fee. This charge varies from $0 to $150, depending on the dealer. It's charged for their administration costs—handling all the paperwork and advertising. Should you pay it? Many dealers insist upon it, going so far as having the fee printed right on their bill of sale forms. Still, you would assume that these regular costs of doing business would be covered in the dealership's overhead. Why should you pay for their paperwork? You can try negotiating on this obviously trumped-up charge, but you won't get much leeway if the management already believes you've been given a good deal. Still, it never hurts to ask.

16. Add-ons. This section is where additional products, like extended warranties and protection packages, are added. You'll be presented to the "business manager," who will try to sell you a whole range of products. Refer to Chapters 8 and 9 for more information on whether you should buy any of these packages.

17. Total vehicle price. This is the sub-total of all charges on which GST will be applied.

18. Trade-in allowance. The value that the dealership has placed on your old car, if you choose to sell it to them. If they have appraised it but you have decided not to sell it to them, make sure this box is empty.

19. Net difference. The cost after the trade-in allowance has been deducted.

20. Provincial sales tax. Check with your dealer. In some provinces, the PST is charged on your purchase price plus the GST. In others, the tax is calculated on the purchase price only.

21. GST on total/sub-total. Your friendly neighbourhood GST!

22. Licence fee. If you are buying new plates you will have to pay the full fee. Check the licensing costs with your provincial Ministry of Transport office, and make sure you aren't being charged an extra fee by the dealership. If you are simply transferring the plates from your old car, a nominal transfer fee is applicable.

23. Fuel. Yes, some dealers will even charge you for filling up the gas tank when you pick up the car. The cost is normally $20, which gets you almost a full tank of regular unleaded. You can specify whatever grade of gasoline you desire. After all, you're paying for it. Some dealers include this free of charge, as a customer service.

You can try to negotiate here. For instance, if you have a trade-in, offer to pay for filling the old car if they pay for the gas in your new one. If they don't agree and insist on charging you for the gas in your new car, you can make a point by bringing along a siphon and a gas can when you drop off your used vehicle. Tell them you'll empty the tank unless they waive the fill-up charge on the new car and see what happens.

24. Payout on liens against trade-in. If there's money still owing on your old car, this is where the final repayment of that debt is calculated and charged against you. Make sure the numbers are correct.

25. Total purchase price. The total cost of everything. Hold on to your seat!

Everything else on the front side is self-explanatory. Make sure the contract is signed by someone with appropriate authority.

Before you sign anything, see that all the details of the transaction are in order and written on the contract. Any special clauses that you want added should be attached to the document, and a note made in the section marked "Remarks" that these extra clauses apply. Don't accept any verbal agreements; they won't hold up well in a court of law.

If you aren't comfortable with signing the document at the dealership, tell the salesperson that you would like to take a copy home and study it. This will allow you to review it in depth, have your lawyer look it over, or show it to your family for their thoughts.

Don't let them bully you into signing before you're ready. If at any point you feel out of control or pressured, get up and leave. Get some fresh air, go for a walk, complain to the general manager, or simply find another dealer.

THE CLAUSES

The bill of sale contains many legal clauses that you should understand before signing the document. Refer to Figure 10.2 for an example of these clauses. They vary little from province to province, so here's a clause-by-clause analysis of our sample bill of sale.

Clause 1: Distance Travelled.   This means that the dealership believes the odometer reading is correct and has not been tampered with. The clause is phrased in a manner that suggests that if this is not the case, it is not the dealer's fault. They have made their best effort to determine this, but do not guarantee the reading. If you're in doubt in the case of a used car, ask to see past service records. Mileage will be recorded on them, and any irregularities will become obvious. This clause also asserts that the odometer on your trade-in has not been tampered with.

Clause 2: Original Pollution Equipment.   This clause asserts that the pollution control equipment on the vehicle you are buying meets the specifications for the model year of the vehicle, that it is intact and that it works as well. This clause also applies to your trade-in. If you know that your emissions equipment is not up to snuff, you should report it to the dealer before signing this agreement. Conversely, if you have been informed by the dealership that your trade requires work to the pollution control equipment, and if this work has been estimated and subtracted from the offer price for your trade-in, make sure that this clause is altered so that it reflects this information.

Clause 3: Safety Standards Certificate and Transfer Documents.   This clause informs you that the vehicle you are purchasing will not be transferred to your name unless you obtain a Safety Standards Certificate from the dealer. Make sure that you ask for this, and make sure that the vehicle is certified at no cost to you. If you neglect to do this, the vehicle may be sold to you with an Unfit Motor Vehicle Permit, which means you cannot drive it until you have obtained a Safety Certificate—you'll have to have the car towed from the dealer's lot, and you'll have to get it safety-certified at your own cost.

Clause 4: Trade-ins.
If you offer your old car as a trade towards partial payment on the new car, this clause states that the car must be in similar condition when you deliver it, less reasonable wear and tear, as it was when the agreement was signed.

The dealer will have inspected your trade and set a price for it during the initial contract signing. If the trade should be involved in an accident, or damaged in some way before the delivery of the new car and exchange of vehicles, then it is your responsibility to complete any repairs.

Clause 5: Manufacturer's Suggested Retail Price.
This clause explains that if the manufacturer raises the suggested retail price of the car you've bought before you take delivery, the dealership can charge the percentage increase to you. In short, if the price goes up, you'll pay.

The clause also tells you that, if you refuse to pay the increase, the dealership has the choice of cancelling the deal or waiving the surcharge.

Don't let it come to that. Have this clause removed from the agreement. If a price has already been agreed on for the car, there's no reason the dealer should be able to charge you more two weeks later. The fact that they've included the option for the dealer to waive this clause shows how difficult it is to enforce.

But don't risk it. Take it out.

Note that the clause covers only price *increases*. What happens if the price goes down? Or if the manufacturer announces a special rebate? There are no clauses in this agreement that allow you to take advantage of situations like this, so you might want to draft one and try to add it.

Clause 6: Payment of Additional and Increased Taxes.
If any federal or provincial tax increases occur between the time you sign this agreement and the time you take delivery, then the contract will be recalculated to include these increases. Unfortunately, there's not much you can do about this clause—taxes are one of those burdens that you just can't get away from without dying first. But, you can include an amendment to this clause that requires the dealer to recalculate the bill of sale in the event of tax *decreases* as well.

Clause 7: Financing Information.
This clause informs you that, if you are financing your car purchase with the dealership on the front of the sales agreement, the dealer complies with provincial regulations regarding consumer protection.

Clause 8: Ownership Transfers Only Upon Payment in Full.
This clause lets you know that

you do not own the vehicle on the front of this contract, nor do you have any partial interest in this vehicle, until the Amount Due on Delivery is paid in full. This is a standard clause, but on this sales contract the clause goes on to repeat portions of Clause 5. Be careful of "loopholes" like this, especially if you go to the trouble of having extra clauses added to the bill of sale. Make sure that all extra clauses that you add to the contract will not be in contradiction of any remaining clauses; otherwise the ones you've added (with the dealer's consent) may be considered invalid.

Clause 9: Delays in the Delivery of the Vehicle.

You are entitled to certain rights under this clause, so it's a good idea to understand it thoroughly.

If the dealer has ordered a new car for you, they have three months to complete delivery. If the car is not ready for you at the end of that time, you will be notified by the dealer that the 90-day period is expiring. Upon notification, you have five days to respond. You have two options

(a) You may agree to extend the contract. This needs to be a mutual agreement, not an arbitrary statement from the dealer that they get more time. You might try to negotiate some concession for extending the agreement. If you decide to extend the deadline, it must be documented in writing and signed by both parties, and must be done before the five days have expired, otherwise the contract is automatically terminated.

(b) You may cancel. If you choose this option, the conditions of Clause 4 come into effect. If the dealership has sold your trade-in during those 90 days (if you gave it to them), then they must refund to you the amount set out on the front of the contract under "Trade-in allowance." If they made a profit on the sale, you see no part of it.

You can have this clause amended to allow the dealership a shorter delivery period. When Kendrew bought a new car in November 1994, he had this clause completely removed from the agreement and added a new clause that allowed the dealership only four weeks to locate and deliver a vehicle to him. His old car was a sport coupe that was not appropriate for winter driving conditions. He was buying a new car because he had moved to an area that experienced heavy snowfalls, and wanted a car he could depend on. The last thing he wanted was to be locked into an agreement that allowed the dealership until late February to find him a new car—he wanted one as soon as possible. If the dealership was unable to complete delivery within four weeks, this allowed Kendrew the option of cancelling the deal and finding something else.

Clause 10: Failure to Accept Delivery or to Pay.

When your car is ready for delivery, you'll be notified by the dealership. Most people look forward to this day, but just in case, the dealership has included this clause. It allows them the right to keep all deposits and traded vehicles if you don't take delivery of the car within seven days of them mailing a notice to you, by prepaid registered mail, to your last known address.

Clause 11: Explanation of Damages.   If the dealer keeps any part of your deposit for "damages," they are required by this clause to provide you with a written document of what the damages are and why you are being charged with them.

Clause 12: Dealing with Trade-ins as Deposits.   This clause explains that if the contract is cancelled before the new vehicle is delivered to the buyer, any vehicle that was given by the buyer to the dealer as a trade-in will be returned under the following conditions.

(a) You have to pay for the Safety Standards Certificate and any administrative costs required to transfer the vehicle back to your name.

(b) You have to pay for any improvements or repairs made to the car by the dealer.

(c) You have to reimburse the dealer for any payments they made to reduce any outstanding liens against your old car.

Extra Clauses

This list is by no means complete: There are dozens of different clauses you may run into, many of which may be designed to protect the dealer but which won't provide much protection for the consumer. Here's a list of some other popular bill of sale clauses.

Acknowledgement of conditions. This clause indicates that you:

(a) have read this entire contract, front and back, and agree to its terms.

(b) agree the contract is not binding unless signed by an authorized agent of the dealership listed on the front of the contract. (Make sure that the document is signed by a sales manager or the general manager of the dealership. Don't let the salesperson convince you that's not necessary.)

(c) will transfer ownership of any trade-in vehicle to the dealer listed on the front of the contract, and that the trade has no liens outstanding other than whatever amounts you have already disclosed.

(d) agree that all information listed on the front of the contract is true.

Warranties. This clause states that no warranties are applicable for this vehicle other than the factory warranty and any listed on the front of the contract. In other words, if you don't have it in writing, forget it! No verbal promises of free oil changes or free service loaner vehicles will be honoured.

Title. This clause explains that the dealer will not deliver the vehicle set out on the front of the contract to the purchaser until the entire purchase price has been paid. It also states that the purchaser must pay any new taxes or increases in current taxes that might come into effect before the vehicle is delivered. So, even if you signed a contract in January, any new taxes from a February federal budget are applicable if you pick up the car in March.

The clause also states that if you are planning to finance all or part of the outstanding balance, and you are unable to obtain the money from any financial institution because of "default or misrepresentation" by you, then the entire purchase price of the car becomes due and payable immediately.

To protect yourself, have an additional clause added to the contract stating that the deal is conditional on your ability to obtain financing. The clause should read as follows: "This contract is void unless the purchaser is able to successfully obtain independent financing for the outstanding balance of the contract."

You can have this clause, and any other additional clauses, prepared by a lawyer if you are concerned about proper wording or loopholes. However, most dealers will cancel a deal if financing is a problem.

Default of payment. If you miss any payments on the vehicle, this clause allows the dealership to immediately demand full payment of the outstanding balance. If you are unable to pay in full, the dealership is allowed to repossess the vehicle and resell it privately or through public auction, making any repairs they deem necessary, and keeping any profits they make (plus whatever payments you'd already made) as "liquidated damages," not as a penalty.

This clause only applies to you if you seek financing through the dealership's financing company. If you've arranged bank financing, then this clause is not relevant.

Cancellation of agreement. If the deal is cancelled by mutual consent of both the purchaser and the dealership, this clause states that the dealer will return any deposits and trades that have been taken in exchange as partial payment for the new vehicle.

In short, anything you've given the dealership is refundable to you immediately upon *mutually agreed* cancellation of the contract. Don't let them try to keep your deposit!

Insurance. This paragraph states that the dealer is not responsible for arranging insurance coverage for your new car. If you haven't arranged any insurance, the dealer cannot be held liable in case of any accidents you might have. The dealer might choose to assist you in arranging insurance if you so request, but this service might come at an additional cost. You're better off doing it yourself.

Only after you've read the contract through completely should you be prepared to sign it. Any additional clauses or changes to current clauses should be attached to the document and referenced in the "Remarks" section. All discounts and concessions should be listed on the front of the document. Make sure all information about you is correct. Use a calculator to check the addition in all columns.

When you are satisfied, sign the document in the required areas. Your signature will need to be witnessed by someone at the dealership, usually your sales representative or the business manager. A signing authority for the dealership also needs to sign.

Make sure you are given a copy of the document with all relevant signatures on it. The dealership should keep a copy as well.

PRIVATE SALES

Several provinces provide sales "kits" to the seller of a privately owned automobile in order to better regulate used-car sales. Often, these kits will include a simple contract that can be signed by both parties.

The most important part of a private sales contract is the legal signing over of the vehicle's ownership papers. Despite what may or may not have been signed prior to this action, unless the ownership papers are signed over by both the buyer and the seller, there is no legal transaction.

If you're buying a vehicle in a private sale, you may want the seller to sign a document that guarantees certain conditions to be true, such as the vehicle having never been involved in an accident.

Finally, if you are unsure at any point about the legal implications of something in the contract, seek professional counsel. As the old saying goes, an ounce of prevention is worth a pound of cure!

QUICK TIPS

SIGNING THE BILL OF SALE

When you buy a car from a dealer, you will sign a sales bill twice. The first time is when you agree to purchase the car and the initial sales form is drawn up. Make sure that it lists all the conditions and figures that you have both agreed to up until this point. It helps to refer to your notes from the negotiations to ensure nothing is missing.

The second bill of sale you will sign will be the official final version, which you will be presented with when you arrive to pick up your car from the dealer. Do not sign this bill of sale until after you have inspected your vehicle and all the paperwork. Ensure that everything meets your approval before you sign the documents.

QUICK TIPS

USED CARS AND THE GST

If you are trading in a less valuable car on the purchase of a car of greater worth, there's a nice new tax twist that benefits the consumer. Goods and services tax (GST) is now credited directly to the value of your older vehicle when trading up to any other type of car, either new or used. Essentially, this means that your old car will now attract a higher trade value than it would have previous- ly. For instance, under the old rules, a consumer living in Ontario would have received a credit of provincial sales tax (PST) only towards the purchase of a new car and the trade-in of an older one. If the trade was valued at $10 000, the credit would have been only $800 (8 percent PST in Ontario). Under the new rules, that same used car would now receive a credit of $1500 (15 percent PST and GST in Ontario). The car itself hasn't changed, but the tax laws have. This means that Canadians receive a slightly higher valuation on their used cars than they did previously. Be aware of this, and ask to be shown the tax credits separately on your bill of sale when trading in for a new or used car. Finally, make sure that the valuation you receive for your used car is accurate and fair based on your research in the Canadian Red Book.

11

Taking It Home

IN THIS CHAPTER:

INSPECTING THE VEHICLE. New or used, when you pick up your car you will want to inspect it one final time before you sign the contracts. This is a necessary step, especially if this is the first time you've seen the vehicle.

THE INSPECTION CHECKLIST. A short check-list to keep you on track during the final inspection.

IF YOU'RE NOT HAPPY. This section offers a number of strategies if everything does not meet your expectations before the final documents are signed.

INSPECTING THE VEHICLE

So you're finally getting ready to pick up your new car! Congratulations. Just don't get so caught up in the excitement that you make mistakes. Sure it's exhilarating, but keep your cool. Once the final bill of sale is signed, there is no going back. Make sure that everything meets your requirements before you pull out a pen.

Make an appointment to pick up your new vehicle with the salesperson who negotiated the deal with you. If you've bought your car at a private sale, arrange a mutually convenient time to pick up the car. You'll need about an hour and a half. Make the appointment during daylight hours, preferably in the middle of a weekday morning, or early morning on a weekend. At dealerships, avoid busy periods when your sales representative might be tempted to cut your time short so that she can deal with other customers.

Bring along notepaper, a pen, a flashlight, your copy of the sales agreement, your driver's licence, proof of insurance, and a certified cheque or money order for the amount due.

When you arrive at the location, let the seller know that you will be inspecting the vehicle first, and completing the paperwork second. Advise her immediately that if everything is not to your satisfaction, you will not be taking delivery.

Whether or not this is your actual intention, saying this advises her that you are aware of your legal rights, as set out in the sales agreement. If the vehicle does not meet with your satisfaction, you have a couple of options, which we'll discuss later in this chapter.

A thorough inspection of the car is absolutely essential, even though it may be time-consuming. Problems that you discover after driving the car home may not be addressed by the seller. At the very least, there could be a dispute as to whether that nick in the paint occurred after the vehicle was driven away by you.

If this is a new car that you're seeing for the first time, follow the checklist provided below. If you're picking up a used car that you've already inspected, give it a once-over to make sure nothing has changed since you last saw it.

New-car buyers often tend to assume that, because the car has never been driven, it will be in perfect condition. As a result, they tend to be somewhat cursory in their inspection.

Big mistake. Even though the odometer shows only 10 clicks, the car may have travelled thousands of kilometres to reach you, in a ship's hold and/or on the back of a truck. Minor, or even major, damage could have occurred along the way. So be very cautious.

Kendrew: I once purchased a demo vehicle from a Toyota dealership. Because of the specific requirements I had, they weren't able to locate a brand new vehicle for me, and I agreed to take delivery of a demonstration model that was being driven by a Toyota executive in Toronto. When I first saw the car the morning I was to pick it up, I discovered a small hole in the trunk lid. When the aftermarket spoiler had been added to the car by the executive, someone had lined up the screw holes poorly, resulting in a hole that they patched up with a strip of duct tape. Of course, I insisted that the trunk lid be repaired properly before I signed the paperwork.

THE INSPECTION CHECKLIST

EXTERIOR INSPECTION

Begin by carefully inspecting the exterior of the car. This is best done during daylight hours, because it is easier to see small scratches or dents in direct sunlight. If the day is overcast or wet, ask to use a service bay or garage. If the dealership has a service drive-through (a driveway that leads directly into the service department counters), use that area if possible. Drive-throughs are better lit and cleaner than service stalls.

Paint   Inspect the paint from bumper to bumper for any shipping scratches, dents, or marks. If found, ask the seller to note any body marks or paint imperfections and initial your comments on the delivery receipt. This is best done in daylight, as night lighting will hide many problems. Use your flashlight to help illuminate shaded areas around the bottom skirt of the vehicle.

Tires   With new cars, check the tire size to ensure they match the size on the specifications sheet. Make sure the spare tire is in its storage area, and that all tools for changing the spare are present.

Lights   Ask the seller to turn on all exterior lights, including flashers and directional signals, while you inspect them from outside the car.

Glass   Examine all window glass for cracks and stone chips that may have occurred during shipping.

> ## QUICK TIPS
>
> **FINDING A PROBLEM**
>
> Whenever you find a problem, make a note of it on your pad, and ask the seller to initial your entry. This reinforces in the salesperson's mind your earlier statement that you may not take delivery of this vehicle, and puts you in a strong position should additional price negotiating become an option.

ENGINE COMPARTMENT

Ask the salesperson to demonstrate how the hood is opened. Using the flashlight, carefully inspect the interior of the body panels for signs of overspray or crumpling. Incidents of dealers trying to resell new cars that have been in accidents are very rare, but can still happen.

Ask the salesperson to explain the engine layout for you so you know where everything is.

Locate the battery and make sure that it is new. If the battery has been replaced with an older one, the casing will appear aged and the labels may be peeling.

If you've ordered any options like ABS or traction control, ask to be shown their location within the engine compartment.

Fluids   Locate the oil dipstick, and check it to make sure that the oil is at the appropriate level. (Believe it or not, new cars have been known to be delivered without oil!) Check the fluid levels for brake, transmission, power steering, and the windshield washers. All should have been topped up by the dealer during the pre-delivery inspection. Ask where, when, and what types of oils and fluids go into the operational machinery, as well as how often the levels should be checked.

TRUNK

Inspect the inner body panels in the trunk for signs of an accident, similar to the exercise explained above. Make sure the salesperson explains any special locking mechanisms or keys that might come with the trunk.

Interior Inspection

Passenger compartment   Look over the seats, dash, door coverings, and the roof liner for correct colour as well as any tears or burns. Carefully examine the roof liner and any fabric that borders the windows for signs of water damage, especially if the vehicle has been shipped from overseas. Make sure that floor mats are present if they've been ordered.

Options   Get out your bill of sale and when sitting in the car, go over the options you ordered. Make sure everything you paid for is there.

Test drive again   Take the car out to make sure it performs as well as the one you test drove originally.

Go over all the controls   Ask the salesperson to explain how the interior controls work, from the headlights, to the windshield wipers, to the radio. You'll find it easier to familiarize yourself with their operation in this way than by reading the manual.

Break-in Period (if new)

Ask the maximum speed at which the car should be driven, and for how long. Also ask whether long-distance driving at the same speed can create problems. Many break-in periods require drivers to vary their speeds every few minutes.

Warranty

Learn the limits of your warranty. Ask for the time or mileage requirement between service periods. Find out if there are any service deductibles on parts or labour. Read Chapter 8 for more information on warranties and extended warranties.

Servicing

You may want to know what services must be performed at the dealership and what can be done by a licensed mechanic without voiding the warranty. More information about servicing your new car is provided in Chapter 12.

THE INSPECTION CHECKLIST

☐ **1. Exterior Inspection**

    ☐ Paint

    ☐ Tires

    ☐ Lights

    ☐ Glass

☐ **2. Engine compartment**

    ☐ Fluids

☐ **3. Trunk**

☐ **4. Interior Inspection**

    ☐ Passenger compartment

    ☐ Options

    ☐ Test drive #2

    ☐ Controls

☐ **5. Break-in Period**

☐ **6. Warranty**

☐ **7. Servicing**

QUICK TIPS

IMPORTING CARS INTO CANADA

There are two sets of federal legislation in Canada that have to be obeyed if you choose to bring in a car from outside our borders. One relates to tariffs and duties, and falls under the jurisdiction of Revenue Canada. The other legislation relates to Transport Canada's Motor Vehicle Safety Act, which governs the safety of the cars on our roads. The first problem you run into is that these two sets of legislation are at odds with each other—in short, they conflict.

The best example of this is Revenue Canada's position on the cars that can be imported into Canada. There are no longer any age restrictions in place. As far as they're concerned, if the vehicle meets the Canadian safety standards, you can pay the duties and bring it on in.

But Transport Canada takes a much different view. They have a substantial list of the cars that can and cannot be brought into Canada, regardless of what Revenue Canada has to say.

So expect to come across some inconsistencies if you choose to pursue this approach.

IF YOU'RE NOT HAPPY

If you aren't satisfied with the condition of the car, you have two options.

1. Do not take delivery of the vehicle being offered. This can be done verbally, but should be followed up in writing. The terms of the standard bill of sale allow this, but give the dealer the right to locate another vehicle for you. If you are refusing delivery of a used car, the contract will probably be cancelled. In that case, don't allow the dealer to keep your money and credit it towards something else on the lot. Once a contract has been nullified, they have no legal right to hold on to your money if you want it back.

2. Re-open negotiations. The dealership may offer some concessions to persuade you to take the car, perhaps an additional discount or an extended warranty. This is the usual course of action under such circumstances. A dealership will not want to nullify a sales contract, so will attempt to sweeten the pot. In this situation, you are in a position of strength. Negotiate for as much as you can possibly get. Always try saying "no" one more time to their "final" offer. You might get a little bit more!

If you are unsure about what to do, refuse delivery until you have time to seek legal counsel. According to the standard bill of sale, delivery can take place any time within three months of the signing date of the contract. If you refuse delivery, the dealership has the option of seeking to enforce the bill of sale legally if they can find an acceptable alternative car. If it comes down to a legal battle, they can usually win— and you don't need the hassle.

The only way out of a signed deal is through negotiation with the dealer (taking another car for the same or similar price), or by finding a legal fault in the contract.

If you need further assistance in terminating a sales agreement, seek legal counsel. Consumer laws differ from province to province, so the best way to know your rights is to speak to a lawyer.

12

Taking Care of the Car

IN THIS CHAPTER:

THE HIGH COST OF REPAIRS. In some situations, repairing your car can be more stressful and more damaging to your wallet than the experience of buying the car in the first place. This section examines the escalating cost of repairs, with some insight into why costs are on the rise and how to find a better deal.

INDEPENDENT GARAGES AND DEALERSHIPS. Where do you take your car for servicing? Can you trust the Mom and Pop service centre on the corner? By the same token, can you trust the Mega-dealership where your car is just one of several hundred they'll see in a single week?

WARRANTY WORK. Whether your car is new or used, there's going to be some kind of warranty attached to it. This section gives tips on how to best take advantage of your warranty.

SECRET WARRANTIES. Although many manufacturers deny their existence, secret warranties are out there. This section tells you what a secret warranty is and how to discover them.

MAKING YOUR CAR LAST FOREVER. Some simple maintenance you can do yourself will greatly extend the life and usability of your car, whether new or used. This section outlines a number of simple maintenance activities you can do in your own driveway.

THE HIGH COST OF REPAIRS

Manufacturers love to sing the praises of their low-maintenance cars that need very little service. Most cars built during this decade have more endurance than their 1980s predecessors. Instead of having to change the spark plugs once a year or clean the carburetor every 10 000 kilometres, with most modern cars you worry only about keeping the fluids topped up and changing the oil every four months. But, for whatever reason, most car owners in Canada still don't maintain their vehicles to the degree today's cars demand.

Failure to practise good maintenance can be costly. Most new cars have warranties that are voided if the manufacturer can prove that you weren't adequately maintaining the car.

When you buy a new car, you'll be given a schedule for recommended servicing. This will include everything from a simple oil change, to checking brake pads, to replacing the timing belt. Following the schedule will keep your warranty valid and keep your car in top operating condition.

Because of the level of sophistication of most new cars, maintenance is best done by qualified mechanics. There are a few things you can do to keep your costs low and your car running well, but most servicing should be done by a professional.

The average price of a new car in North America has topped the $20 000 mark. Much of this high cost is because of new technologies like airbags, ABS, side impact beams, upgraded suspensions, and better steering systems. Automobiles now have more computers in them than the average household. So it's not as easy as it used to be to just pop open the hood and start tinkering with the engine. Even service departments will admit that new technologies make it harder for them to do their jobs. Complex tools and computerized diagnostic systems need to be purchased to service many new cars. This is one of the reasons why many corner service stations can't do much more than a simple oil change—the cost of keeping up with technology quickly becomes an insurmountable obstacle.

Of course, the high cost of all this equipment isn't just absorbed by the service centres that can afford them. It's passed on to you. It's painfully apparent, as soon as you walk into a dealership service department, that their charges are going to be higher than independent garages. All you have to do is look for their billing sign and compare their hourly rate with that of your local garage. The dealership will be anywhere from 25 to 50 percent more expensive.

So why go there if it's more expensive?

You can't escape these higher costs by buying an older car that doesn't contain any advanced computer systems. Any money you save on complicated servicing requirements you'll quickly lose again through more frequent trips to your mechanic. As a general rule of thumb, the older your car is, the more often you'll have to take it into the shop.

Depending on the type of car you buy, the service requirements might be so sophisticated that you'll have to visit a dealership to get the work done. Smaller garages won't have the proper know-how and equipment.

But you don't *always* have to go to a dealership. Canadians are big believers in the myth that warranty maintenance schedules can only be met by a manufacturer-approved dealer. That's just not true. Many manufacturers will honour your warranty even if you never have any scheduled maintenance work performed at an authorized dealer. The trick is to find out what stipulations they'll apply to this.

INDEPENDENT GARAGES AND DEALERSHIPS

The vehicle service industry is highly competitive these days. It's estimated that about 75 percent of vehicle owners stop taking their cars to the manufacturer's dealership for servicing once the warranty expires. And it appears more people are catching on to the idea that warranty maintenance work can be done at smaller garages. The manufacturers recognize this trend, and they've started to fight back.

And so they should. With the high price of new cars, Canadians are keeping their cars longer. Vehicle servicing has become a very large industry—Canadians now spend over $12 billion a year maintaining their cars.

No doubt you've seen the GM commercials singing the praises of their service departments. Did you notice that the commercials weren't advertising a new car or truck? Instead, GM emphasized the launch of their new Five Star service program, and tried promoting their service departments instead of their new-car division. Obviously the managers are waking up to the fact that there's big money to be made in vehicle service.

Used-car buyers have the upper hand when it comes to making choices between independents and dealerships. If you buy your used car from an established dealer, you'll probably be offered a short-term warranty on the car (between three months and one year). If the warranty is free with the purchase of the used car, then you have complete freedom to service the car wherever you want. You can negotiate this warranty, changing the term or the cost of the service. Your negotiating tool is servicing your vehicle at the dealer where you're purchasing the car. Tell them that if they want your service business, they need to earn it with a free warranty (or a better warranty). This isn't a guaranteed negotiating strategy—it only works at a limited number of dealers. But it can't hurt to try it out.

If you buy a new car, you'll likely be told by your sales representative that you really have little choice but to service your car at the dealer where you bought it. Sure, you can probably go to another dealership, but why jump from dealer to dealer when it's best to keep your business in one locale? That's how the argument will run.

In fact, you *do* have another choice. Independent garages have been around since the first car rolled off the assembly line, and with careful hunting you'll find better quality service for a much better price.

When you visit the service department of the dealership where you buy your new car, specifically ask the manager where you can have regular maintenance performed. In many cases, any CAA-approved service shop will do—and most will be cheaper than going through the dealership.

If the service manager is unhelpful (after all, you're asking him or her to recommend a competitor), check with CAA to see which garages they recommend in your area. Ask friends and neighbours where they service their car. Look in the Yellow Pages under Garages—Auto Repairing. Try to find a garage that specializes in your make of car, especially if it's an imported vehicle. They will usually have the needed specialized tools and they'll be able to recognize common problems that occur with your make and model.

Any regularly scheduled maintenance work that is done at an independent garage should be well documented. You don't want any hassles if you require work to be done under warranty at the dealership. Make sure the maintenance schedule is followed as closely as possible.

Price is one big negative with dealership servicing. Another is the fairly regular practice of performing unnecessary maintenance on a car by misdiagnosing the problem. This happens surprisingly often.

Dealership service departments are set up to extract as much profit as possible from the consumer. That's not to say you won't get a good deal through a dealership service department; you just need to be careful.

Dealerships usually employ service advisers, who act as the liaison between the mechanics and the consumer. The service adviser listens to your problems, writes up the work order for the car, assigns it to one of several crews he or she might have working under them, and schedules times when customers can drop off their cars for service. Many service advisers are paid on a commission basis. That means it's in their best interest to get the service crew to work as quickly and efficiently as possible. The faster the turn-around time, the more cars that can be run through the service bays—and the more income they earn.

Many service departments charge according to a flat-rate billing system. The rationale is that the consumer won't get over-charged because a crew spends hours dawdling on a single car. Instead, each job is charged after consulting a manual provided by the manufacturer. The manual lists all the service work that can be performed on a specific car, and tells the mechanic how long that job should take to complete. If the manual says it will take two hours, that's what you'll be charged—even if the job only takes forty minutes.

This can be advantageous to you if your car is old. New cars have new parts, so repairs can normally be completed fairly quickly. Older cars have parts that may be seized or fused, that might be covered with years of oil and grime, or that might be rusted into place. So jobs on older cars often take longer to complete than the times recommended in the manual.

If your service department is honest, they'll charge you by the manual times, even if the job took a lot longer. This can save you a lot of money.

But this is also why you'll run into problems with misdiagnosis at a dealership. The service adviser wants to push through as many cars as possible so he or she can collect the commissions. The mechanics are told to work quickly so that more cars can be serviced. Therefore, no one really takes time to analyse what might be causing a specific problem, especially if it's complex. The crew reads the work order, and completes the job. Occasionally, it's the wrong job.

Kendrew: I had a problem like this with my first car, a 1988 Toyota Corolla GTS. During the summer of 1993, I began to notice a bluish white smoke that would billow from the left front wheel well when the car was stopped at red lights, or after long-distance driving. As you'd imagine, this was quite disconcerting.

My first visit to a dealership service department resulted in my being told the problem was a build-up of gravel and dirt in the brake lining of the left front wheel. The brake was taken apart, cleaned, and reassembled. New brake linings were installed. Total cost: $320.

A few days later the problem showed up again. The smoke was just as thick, and appeared under the same circumstances. I took the car back for another look. This time it was explained that the brake was not functioning properly at all, and the entire brake assembly would need to be replaced. Total cost: $575.

The problem reappeared three months later. By that time, I had decided just to sell the car and save myself the hassle. One day, while I was stopped at a small garage in northern Ontario for a fill-up, the attendant commented on the bluish white smoke billowing from the car's wheel well. He suggested that the problem could be an oil leak on the hot engine. Three days later the problem was repaired, and never resurfaced. Total cost: $35.

Maybe there was a problem with the brake assembly. Or maybe the service adviser was just guessing. But I was left to wonder whether anyone ever checked for an oil leak, or whether the adviser was just making an educated guess at the problem based on the description I gave him, and the crew just slavishly followed the directions on the work order.

WARRANTY WORK

You will no doubt have some warranty work done on your car, especially if you purchase an extended warranty. Warranties are so long these days that it's pretty well guaranteed that a claim will be made on most cars under three years of age.

Your warranty work is never completely free, no matter what you're told. The part being repaired is covered under warranty. So is the labour. But you may have to pay for any new gaskets or seals or screws or grease—anything that is needed during the work that isn't specifically covered by the warranty. Remember, those items deteriorate under normal wear and tear, which is a condition of your warranty. There's nothing illegal or unethical about charging you for the replacement of these parts. So find out exactly what work is being done to your car, and what costs will be involved. Usually, they'll be minimal, but it's a good idea to ask.

In many instances, warranty claims will begin to mount on a car in the third or fourth year, which is when parts will begin to fail as a result of wear and tear. Take advantage of those opportunities to have other work done at a cheaper price.

Kendrew: I had some warranty work done on a Corolla. At the time, the car was about 10 000 kilometres away from scheduled maintenance that required the replacement of the timing belt in the engine. This is normally a fairly expensive job, as the engine has to be partially dismantled to get at the belt.

I asked what work was being done under warranty, and if there was anything else that could be worked on at the same time. It turned out that the warranty work was being done on a part of the engine that was close to the timing belt. I arranged to have the belt replaced at the same time. I paid for the purchase of the part, but saved money on the labour because the warranty work covered it. So, a job that would have cost several hundred dollars ended up costing about seventy.

When your car goes in for warranty work, make a point of asking what other work could be done at the same time.

SECRET WARRANTIES

Have you ever heard of people who went into a dealership service department with a problem and screamed so loudly they got it fixed at no cost? It happens often. These are consumers who are taking advantage of secret warranties.

Secret warranties are implemented when a problem occurs with a large number of cars in a specific product line. The problem is obviously a defect, but a recall would cost the manufacturer hundreds of millions of dollars. Instead, the company quietly authorizes dealerships to repair the problem at a reduced rate, or, sometimes, free of charge, if the customer fusses enough. Manufacturers and dealerships call these "goodwill" repairs. But in reality there's no good will involved. It's a case of getting out of a difficult situation at minimal cost.

These policies are kept secret, hidden from the consumer. As a result, many people end up paying hundreds, even thousands of dollars to repair a problem that they have no idea is, in fact, a defect. Dealers won't say a word unless the consumer complains first.

Some secret warranties have recently been "outed." No manufacturer is exempt: It turns out that secret warranties exist across the board, for both domestic and imported automobiles. Here's some examples of recent secret warranties.

Ford had a "limited service program" that applied to rust problems on 12 million 1969–72 cars and trucks. The program was described to Ford regional offices as "a limited service program without dealership notification [which] should be administered on an individual complaint basis." Under the program, Ford would pay up to 100 percent of repair costs resulting from rust damage.

In 1994, Ford had a similar "limited service program" that covered peeling paint on 1985–92 cars and trucks. F Series pick-up trucks from this period experienced the most extensive peeling paint problems because Ford skipped the primer layer when painting the trucks.

Mazda had a secret warranty in 1972 that doubled the warranty coverage for their rotary engines, the engines used in all Mazda RX-7 sports cars.

1983–1986 Toyota Camrys had a secret warranty that covered problems with pulsating brakes.

The list could go on: It's estimated that there are presently hundreds of secret warranties issued by all the major manufacturers to cover defects on all of their current vehicles. With the rapid advancements in computerized components in modern cars, it's conceivable that there are secret warranties that exist to cover problems with advanced systems like ABS, airbags, traction control, and other technologies.

Trying to uncover a secret warranty is a lot like trying to find a vintage used car with less than 1000 kilometres on the odometer. It takes a lot of luck and persistence and research. Not surprisingly, manufacturers keep their secret warranties extremely well guarded. In fact, many manufacturers will publicly deny any existence of secret warranties at all. This is a shady practice that benefits the manufacturer at the buyer's expense, and should come to an end.

But no matter how loudly consumer advocacy groups complain, the practice of secret warranties still persists. During the 1980s, General Motors front-wheel-drive compacts and mid-size cars were built with defective rack and pinion steering assemblies that would begin to freeze up after about 85 000 kilometres. The problem will be repaired (either partly or completely free, depending on how loudly you can yell) by any GM dealer. The catch is that you have to pay the labour costs. If this were a real warranty claim, those costs would be free.

Finding a secret warranty requires a great deal of work and patience. Unfortunately, there is no legislation currently in place in Canada to aid the process, although a few American states have enacted secret warranty laws that protect consumers. Until that happens in Canada, it's up to each individual consumer to uncover whatever information they can.

First, check out the technical service bulletins at your dealership's service department for news about your specific vehicle. Service bulletins are published by the manufacturer and sent to the dealerships whenever there is a common problem with a specific vehicle or model class. Service bulletins won't prove the existence of a secret warranty, since they cover everything from common problems to new repair techniques. But by scrutinizing the bulletins that pertain to your vehicle, you can sometimes uncover clues that can point you in the right direction.

Keep your eye out for a service bulletin that tells the dealer how to diagnose and fix a defect, and that will also authorize the dealer to make repairs at the manufacturer's expense. It's very rare to come across a service bulletin that states this so obviously. You're more likely to come across statements about "goodwill assistance" or "limited service offer." Statements like this often shroud a secret warranty that you can use to your advantage. To get your hands on the service bulletins available for your vehicle, contact the service department at your dealer. If this is unsuccessful, try contacting the manufacturer directly.

Another way to uncover a secret warranty is by communicating with other owners of vehicles similar to yours—same manufacturer, model, and age. Common problems that you discover through communicating with other owners may be common enough to have forced the manufacturer to initiate a secret warranty. You can find other owners of cars similar to yours by visiting the waiting room at the service centre you use, or by posting messages in Internet discussion groups that pertain to your vehicle.

To use a suspected secret warranty for repairs to your car, you'll get top results if you have a copy of a service bulletin that alludes to the existence of the common defect. If you have such a document, your task is made much easier. You'll still get some resistance, but much less than if you go in empty-handed.

But sometimes it's impossible to find any written documentation of the problem you suspect might be a common defect. In these situations, your best recourse is to team up with other consumers experiencing the same problem and apply pressure as a group to both the dealership and the manufacturer. In some cases you may need legal counsel. If you suspect your vehicle is defective in some way, but are having trouble proving it, contact the Automobile Protection Association (APA).

For more detailed information about secret warranties (although from an American perspective), read *Little Secrets of the Automobile Industry* by Clarence Ditlow and Ray Gold (Emeryville, CA: Moyer Bell, 1994).

MAKING YOUR CAR LAST FOREVER

With the dramatic advances in automotive technology, there is no reason why your car shouldn't last many years if you maintain it properly.

If you maintain it properly—that's the key. A well-maintained car will last the owner for ten, fifteen, twenty or more years. A poorly maintained car will be in the junk yard inside of eight years.

North Americans are conditioned to believe that once a car hits 100 000 kilometres, it's time to get rid of it. It's true that the 100 000- to 150 000-kilometre mark is usually about the time that major components begin to wear out. But if you've bought a reliable car with a reliable engine, you should enjoy many years of good driving once you get past this hump. Kendrew remembers a Toyota Corolla, like his, that showed up at his dealership's service drive-through one summer morning. Curious about the mileage on it, he glanced at the odometer. It registered over 300 000 kilometres!

The greatest obstacle to making your car last forever is rust. Rust is the cancer of the automobile; once it gets in, there's no getting it out.

In most parts of Canada, cars are exposed to conditions that encourage rust formation. Using salt on our roads is good for melting ice, but is rough on car bodies. Salt helps oxidize the metal, which is what causes rust.

You should consider rust proofing your car if you intend on driving it during the winter months. Many cars now come with factory rust proofing, but the job may not be complete without after-market work (see Chapter 9 for more information).

Some other tips to keep rust at bay:

1. Get some touch-up paint from a dealership or at any automotive accessories store and immediately cover up any chips that expose the sheet metal beneath the paint coats.

2. Rinse your car with fresh water often during the winter months, maybe once or twice a week. You don't need a full car wash, just a spray-down that will remove salt buildups from the surface. Many dealerships have pressure sprays that you might be able to use free of charge. There are also many self-serve wash bays across our country where, for a loonie or two, you can wash your car in a heated stall with clean warm water. This is highly recommended.

3. Wax your car at least twice a year: once in the spring, to protect it against bird droppings and sap that might drip from nearby trees, and once in the fall to protect the finish during the winter months. Of course, wax looks great on a new car, so you might want to do it more often, but that's up to you.

It doesn't take much, just a little bit of tender loving care to keep your car looking clean and young. And, the better it looks, the more money you'll get for it when it comes time to sell.

Another important aspect of maintenance is tire maintenance. Well-maintained tires will benefit every aspect of your driving, from braking to handling to road noise. Here are some maintenance tips.

- Pressure them. Check the tire pressure monthly. Do so when the tires are cold, after the car has been sitting quietly for a few hours. Overinflated tires will wear out faster down the centre line of the tread. They'll also provide dramatically less traction and braking control. Underinflation results in similar control problems, but the wear will be most evident on the sides of the tread. If your tires are already showing any of these wear signs, it might be attributable to inflation problems.

- Inspect them. Check the tread when you're checking your tire pressure. The grooves should be deep enough that you can't feel the bottom with your fingertip (unless you have very thin fingers!). Any shallower than that, and they'll need replacing. If you find any lodged stones or pieces of glass, remove them with the tip of your car key.

- Even them out. Tires wear faster depending on whether your car is front- or rear-wheel drive. Rotating your tires swaps them front and back, and sometimes side to side, depending on your mechanic's philosophy. Rotate your tires every 15 000 km.

- Baby them. Avoid hard cornering, wheel-spinning acceleration, sudden braking, and extraordinarily high speeds. Be aware of your tires' speed rating, and don't exceed it.

QUICK TIPS

DECIPHERING TIRE CODES

One of the hardest parts of the tire-buying process is decoding all the writing and symbols that appear along the tire's sidewall. There's a wealth of information there, but it's usually just gobble-de-gook to most of us.

A relatively generic tire might read as follows: Firestone FR721   P175/80 R13 M+S   Max load 535 kg 1170 lbs at 240 Kpa (35 psi) max press   DOT W2JU F75 146

Breaking the code isn't hard. The line above contains the following information.

Manufacturer and model. In this case, the tire is a Firestone FR721. Tire size. The "P" indicates that this is a passenger tire. "175," the number immediately following the "P," tells you the width of the tire's cross section in millimetres. The number "80" is the tire's aspect ratio, which is the ratio of the height of the sidewall to the cross section width. Generally, the larger this number is, the larger the tire sidewall is. In this case, the tire is 80 percent as high as it is wide. The aspect ratio will give you an idea of how the tire will handle cornering and traction. "R" stands for radial in this case, and the number following it, "13," tells you the diameter of the tire in inches.

Speed rating. On this tire, the speed rating is "M+S." Speed ratings tell you what top speeds the tire can endure without failure. "S" tires are rated to 180 km/h.

Load and pressure. "Max load 535 kg 1170 lbs" tells you how much weight this tire can carry safely at its recommended inflation pressure ("at 240 Kpa (35 psi) max press"). Given that you have four tires, it's exceedingly rare to surpass the load ratings. Just make sure your tires are always properly inflated.

Manufacturing date. The DOT serial number tells you where the tire was made and when. Codes for tire plants differ from brand to brand, but the date of construction can be read in a small rectangular depression in the side of the tire following the DOT. The first two numbers tell you the week of the year. In this case, the number 146 tells you the tire was made during the fourteenth week of 1996.

13

Driveway Dealership

IN THIS CHAPTER:

THE PROS AND CONS OF SELLING IT YOURSELF

You'll make considerably more money selling your old car privately than by trading it in to a dealership. Dealers sell their cars at retail prices, but buy them at wholesale. This gives them a potential profit margin of several thousand dollars. That money can just as easily go into your own pocket, if you're willing to accept the nuisances involved in selling your car privately. Here's what you'll be up against.

SAFETY

You'll be advertising your name and phone number in a city- or province-wide publication. People interested in your vehicle will call, get directions to your home, and show up to look at the vehicle. But what if callers are more interested in determining where you live and how easy it might be to break into your home? Granted, this is a long shot, but it can be a source of concern for older couples, single women, or anyone who is wary of inviting strangers to visit their home or drive their car.

Counter-action: Set the meeting place in the parking lot of a local school or mall. Don't go alone—bring along a friend or relative. There is safety in numbers.

TIME

It takes a lot of time to sell a car. Dealerships usually have a turnover period of about three months between the time they receive a used car and the time they can sell it. If you're still financing your old vehicle, this can be costly, especially if you're already making payments on a new one.

You also have to be prepared to tie up your weekends and/or evening hours showing the car to prospective buyers. This could put pressure on your family time, especially when you set aside several hours to show your car to someone who never shows up, or arrives late, say during dinner.

COSTS

Your costs might run from a simple "For Sale" sign to expensive ads in newspapers and magazines. You'll also need to have the car professionally cleaned and certified. There might be minor repairs needed for certification that will eat into your profit margin. These costs will be multiplied by the time factor. If it takes six months to sell your car, you'll be paying for advertising during that entire period.

NEGOTIATING

You'll have to go through the stress of negotiations again, this time as the seller. You'll have to deal with unreasonable demands from customers, low offers, and general haggling. Put yourself in the position of a buyer again. You were looking for a top quality car in good condition, at the best possible price. This is what to expect from the people who visit you. You'll begin to understand what a professional car salesperson goes through every day. In fact, you might want to sell your own car before buying a new one. That may leave you temporarily without wheels but you might pick up some new negotiating tricks from your potential buyers.

TIPS ON GETTING TOP DOLLAR

Keep two objectives in mind when selling your old car.

1. You want to move it as quickly as possible.

2. You want the most money you can get for it.

To achieve both objectives, you'll need a sales strategy. You can't expect to put a sign in the car window and hope someone will see it. This occasionally works, but you'll get better results by following a well-thought-out plan. Here are some recommended sales techniques

Sell your car when it will be most in demand. Trying to sell a convertible sports car at the beginning of December will virtually guarantee you a long sale period, and you'll probably have to settle for a lower price. Equally, selling a four-wheel-drive sport utility vehicle won't attract as much attention in July as it will in November.

Advertise your vehicle in high-exposure areas. Local newspapers are a good choice. There are also several automobile buy and sell publications in Canada, some of which specialize in imports, older domestics, trucks, and even motorcycles. These publications are widely read by enthusiasts, dealers, and regular folk looking for their next car. Advertising costs are reasonable.

Prepare a good advertisement. A good ad will attract attention and generate traffic to look at your car. It should include the following elements.

(a) The year and model of the vehicle.

(b) A physical description of the exterior.

(c) "Hot buttons" that set it apart from other similar cars and will excite a potential buyer.

(d) The asking price. Do not indicate it's negotiable.

(e) Your first name (not your last), phone number, and a decent time to call.

Here are a few sample ads from *Auto Trader* magazine.

(a) This ad appeals to shoppers looking for a no-nonsense car that has been well kept. Notice how the advertiser points out "lady driven" and "clean inside & out."

1993 Ford Tempo. Grey silver, 4 dr, air, auto, 4 cyl, 73 000 km, lady driven, clean inside & out. Asking $8000.

(b) Here's a good ad for a newer luxury car. Here the advertiser has hit the "hot buttons" for exclusivity ("top of the line, loaded") and a clean car ("excellent condition"):

1996 Buick Regal Grand Sport. Top of the line & absolutely loaded, leather, dual P/seats, CD player & power moonroof. Excellent condition.

(c) If you're a student or someone looking for low-cost transportation, here's an ad that will appeal directly to you:

1995 Geo Metro. All original economical transportation. 3 cyl engine with std. trans., P/trunk, fold down rear seats, special body decal pkg, new clutch! Excellent value! $6995.

The more potential buyers your ad generates, the better your chances of selling your car quickly. So consider your ad as your first line of attack in your sales campaign. Make sure it does its job well by designing it to attract as many callers as possible.

"Hot buttons" are what automotive salespeople use to help make a customer more interested in a vehicle. You can do the same, by figuring out what type of people would be most interested in your vehicle and designing an ad that appeals to them with the use of "hot buttons."

For instance, if you're selling your old Mazda RX-7 sport coupe, you know that the most interest in your ad will come from people looking for a sports car. The "hot buttons" here will probably be performance, acceleration, speed, and classic styling. Accentuate these aspects of your car by specifically mentioning "superior performance" or "superb handling" in your ad.

Alternatively, if you're selling your family wagon, stress safety features, reliability, and storage capacity. You know what your target market is—play to it.

Take another look at sample ad (b). The target market here is people looking for luxury at an affordable price. This would probably be an older couple, perhaps retired, living on a modest income. Notice how these "hot buttons" are played to.

Convert callers to viewers. Once you've placed your ad, don't sit back and wait for customers to beat a path to your door. Remember, this is only the first line of attack. You want to transform all callers into actual physical presences. No one is going to buy the car over the telephone—they need to come see it before they'll decide.

When you start getting callers, don't just answer their questions about the vehicle and hang up. Once they've got the basic information, it's too easy to decide against buying your car without even seeing it. Use some sales skills. Talk up the good points of the car. Stress the advantages and the features. Interest them.

Never volunteer any negative information over the phone if you can help it. You can't lie to a direct question, but you don't need to answer questions that are never asked. Don't discuss what needs to be done to certify it. Stay positive.

Get as much information from the caller as possible. Use some of the tricks you've experienced at dealerships to do this.

Arrange an appointment. Don't ask callers when they might come, tell them. Say there's a lot of interest in the vehicle and you'll be showing it tomorrow evening. If that's convenient, they can come by around eight. You can use this technique with any day, any time.

Write down the caller's name and phone number so that you can be in touch if something comes up. Tell them you want this information so you can call if the car gets sold before their appointment. That will make them more anxious, and provide you with their name and number so you can follow up if they're late or don't show.

Don't discuss price over the phone. If the buyer wants to negotiate over the telephone, tell them that you aren't prepared to discuss price until you know they're legitimately interested in the vehicle. Point out they can't decide that until they see it. Don't let them tell you they don't know if they're "legitimately interested" until they know the price. Tell them that the price is as listed unless mutually agreed otherwise—after they've seen the car.

Show off the car. Show the car in the most creative way possible to stimulate immediate interest. Here are some tips from Mel, who's had a great deal of experience showing cars in private sales.

(a) Sports cars. Get your car cleaned inside and out, with a nice wax job and polished tires. Add a performance-boosting solution to the gasoline, like "Octane Boost" from Canadian Tire. This will make the car peppier and smoother during test drives.

If you can get a car cover, put the vehicle into your garage and cover it up. When people come to see it, they'll be led into a warm garage, where they'll see the car covered and protected. The last thought in their minds will be whether or not this car was abused. Instead, they'll think they've found a collector's item!

(b) Family cars. Again, get the car cleaned, especially if you've been carrying a family in it for several years. The "Hot Buttons" for family-oriented buyers are things like safety, roominess, and reliability, so stop at the gas station and make sure the tires are fully inflated. Invest some money in having the brake pads replaced, or the brakes tuned, so that test drivers will feel confident in your car's safety. Have as many of the service records as possible on hand. You'll want to show them to potential buyers as evidence of reliability.

Show the car outdoors during sunny days, not at night. Natural light will help make the car appear roomier, bettering your chances for a sale.

Accentuate the positive. In the automotive industry, it's said that every car has a story. Make your car's story as appealing as possible to potential buyers. Remember, the show is one of the most important parts of the deal.

Under no circumstances should you ever lie about your car to customers. Anything you say can come back to haunt you if you are dishonest. Be up front and truthful at all times. If your price is realistic, you'll find a buyer—perhaps faster than you ever expected!

14

Insurance

IN THIS CHAPTER:

HOW INSURANCE WORKS. Every driver in Canada is required by law to carry insurance for their automobile in case of an accident. Automobile accidents are the leading cause of death among human beings in North America. It's no wonder that we are required to protect ourselves financially from others. This section explains how auto insurance works and how it can benefit your driving experience.

INSURANCE REQUIREMENTS FOR CANADIANS. Every province has different insurance requirements. This section tells you what you need and what you don't need, province by province.

SIX TIPS TO LOWER PREMIUMS. If you want lower insurance premiums (and who doesn't), read these six tips to reducing your costs.

FILING A CLAIM. We all hope it won't happen to us, but statistics show that every driver in Canada will experience at least two minor car accidents during their driving career. This section shows you how to make an efficient insurance claim, ensuring that you receive your money in the fastest time possible.

HOW INSURANCE WORKS

Regardless of where you live in Canada, one rule applies equally to all car owners: If you own and drive a car on public roads, you are required by law to carry auto insurance. Insurance protects you and every other driver on the road. Cars are driven by human beings, and we tend to make mistakes. A fender-bender can cost as much as $3000 in damage, which isn't a good way to start the week. Insurance can take care of the damages without stinging your wallet, but only if you've got a policy you can depend upon. Just like shopping for a dependable car, shopping for auto insurance is a better experience when you know what you're looking for and where to get it at a good price.

Let's start our examination of the topic by looking at the concept of auto insurance itself. Insurance is essentially a guarantee or warranty. The issuing company promises to protect you from the financial trauma of damage to your vehicle. Auto insurance carries three distinct guarantees:

1. Collision. You are guaranteed not to have a collision with another vehicle or object. If you do, the insurance company will pay for the repairs to your car and compensate you for any lost wages resulting from injuries.

2. Liability. You are guaranteed not to be held liable for any trauma caused to others as a result of any collisions you might have. The insurance company will assume your liability, up to a predetermined point. Let's assume a situation in which you have liability insurance of $1 million. You crash your car through the front window of someone's house during their daughter's wedding, and they sue for $1 million. In this case, the insurance company will pay the damages of the lawsuit, unless the judge awards more than $1 million to the plaintiff, in which case you are responsible for any amount over your coverage.

3. Comprehensive. This facet of auto insurance covers fire and theft. If your car is damaged or destroyed as a result of either fire or theft (including vandalism), your insurance company will assume replacement or repair costs.

INSURANCE REQUIREMENTS FOR CANADIANS

Depending on the province you live in, you'll be required to carry some or all of these components on your personal auto insurance. Here's the breakdown.

Province	Comprehensive	Collision	Liability	Accident Benefits
British Columbia	Optional	Optional	Mandatory	Mandatory
Alberta	Optional	Optional	Mandatory	Mandatory
Saskatchewan	Optional	Mandatory	Mandatory	Mandatory
Manitoba	Optional	Mandatory	Mandatory	Mandatory
Ontario	Optional	Optional	Mandatory	Mandatory
Quebec	Optional	Optional	Mandatory	Mandatory
New Brunswick	Optional	Optional	Mandatory	Mandatory
Nova Scotia	Optional	Optional	Mandatory	Mandatory
PEI	Optional	Optional	Mandatory	Mandatory
Newfoundland	Optional	Optional	Mandatory	Optional

SIX TIPS TO LOWER PREMIUMS

Because insurance has become more expensive in recent years, many consumers are looking for ways to reduce their premiums. Most choose the simplest route: They cut back on their amount of coverage. This can involve reducing some or all of the components of insurance in a policy, or even eliminating certain ones altogether. But there are better options.

Insurance is based on actuarial science. Your first step in cutting costs is to recognize that actuarial science is based on two elements: historical data and predictions of what will happen based on historical data. Knowing this, you can cut your costs in the following ways.

1. Purchase and insure a used car. Insurance premiums are based on how much it will cost to replace your vehicle if it is stolen or destroyed. By lowering your replacement cost, you lower your premiums. A $10 000 used car will cost less to insure than a $25 000 new car.

2. Drive a car with low accident statistics and cheap repair bills. Driving a Pontiac Trans-Am or any other high testosterone sports car will raise your rates, simply because these vehicles tend to be driven (quickly) by aggressive young men. Consequently, they are involved in more accidents. Your insurance company will charge you a lot of money for the luxury of driving such a car. Shop carefully for a vehicle that is common enough on the road that parts are easy to find. Also, avoid limited-market vehicles such as Volvo or Saab. Repair costs are higher on them because parts are more difficult to obtain and are more costly. When choosing your next vehicle, keep in mind this graph as a way to trim your insurance costs.

INSURANCE GRADATION SCALE

Higher

Sports Cars
Premium Coupes
Premium Sedans
Sport Utility Vehicles
Sport Coupes
Minivans
Pick-up Trucks
Sedans

Lower

3. Provide your insurance company with as much information as possible that supports a lower insurance rating. For instance, Toronto is an expensive place to drive a car — there are many car accidents and a great deal of theft and vandalism. If you inform your insurance agent that you live in Toronto, your rates will be adjusted upwards to reflect the higher-risk location of your vehicle. But, if you advise your insurance agent that you actually live in Richmond Hill, north of Toronto, you'll place yourself in a potentially lower-rated locale.

We are not suggesting that you include false information on your insurance application. If you report that you live in Winnipeg, Manitoba in an effort to reduce your rates, but you have three accidents in downtown Toronto, you could face charges of insurance fraud. Insurance agents will want to know where and by whom the vehicle is being driven.

4. List a lower-rated person as the primary driver. For instance, if you are a 25-year-old man married to a 27-year-old woman, it would be in your best interest to list your wife as the primary driver of the vehicle and yourself as a part-time or occasional driver. Your 27-year-old wife will attract a lower insurance premium than you will. Again, don't lie. If your wife is to be listed as the primary driver, then she must be the primary driver.

5. Maintain a good driving record. Report moving violations and car accidents to your insurance company when they occur. Although policies differ among insurance companies, violations such as speeding tickets will stay on your insurance record for five years, and traffic accidents for as long as seven. Ask questions about this when you are shopping for a good policy.

6. Shop for the best insurance rate. Use all of the resources at your disposal. Start by contacting an insurance broker, but also get two or three quotations of your own from insurance companies. Quotations will differ wildly from one company to the next. Every company has different experiences handling claims, and their premiums differ as a result. They also employ their own captive staff of actuaries. A broker can help you navigate the maze of insurance companies by shopping several companies on your behalf. You provide the necessary information, and the broker collects quotations. Although the broker should present you with the best quotation possible, if you're at all concerned it helps to have done some independent research.

QUICK TIPS

INSURANCE II

Insurance companies use teams of actuaries working for them to determine the odds for and against different types of automotive costs. They consider historical data for different categories, and come to a mathematical expression of how likely you are to file a claim during the life of your policy and how much that claim is likely to be. The data they use is compiled from anyone who matches certain criteria with you, and can go back several decades. For instance, if you are a male driver between the ages of 16 and 25, you will pay higher insurance premiums than a man or woman in his or her mid-40s. Regardless of your personal vehicle history, your rates are based on the experiences of every other male driver in your age range in Canada. This is discrimination, but it's the way insurance works. It may not be fair, but your only option is to refuse to purchase auto insurance, which makes it illegal for you to drive your vehicle. The industry has a stranglehold on the Canadian public.

FILING A CLAIM

Obtaining low insurance premiums is only half the game, however. It's one thing to obtain insurance. It's another thing to have to use it. Many drivers are afraid to use their insurance policies. They worry that small claims will increase their premiums. When fender-benders and other minor incidents occur, a surprising number of consumers will choose to pay for repairs themselves rather than use their insurance policy. This seems ludicrous at first glance. Why pay several hundred (or even thousand) dollars a year only to then pay for damages out of your own pocket?

But while it may seem ludicrous, it is also a good strategy. Insurance premiums do increase when claims are made. Save your insurance use for when you really need it. When a major accident does occur, there are several steps you should be aware of. Most drivers are unfamiliar with what happens after a major accident has occurred, and as a result can often fall victim to deceit in the vehicle-repair industry.

If you suffer a major accident, your first priority is to ensure the safety and health of all passengers in your vehicle, as well as the drivers and passengers in any other vehicles involved in the accident. If a police officer is called to the scene, record his or her name and badge number. Also record the time of the accident and the location, and write a detailed account of the circumstances that caused the accident as soon as is reasonably possible. If you've been taken from the scene by ambulance (which is fairly common, even with minor injuries), find out the name and badge number of the police officer assigned to the scene and follow up with him or her as soon as you can. Your car will most likely be removed from the scene by tow truck (if it's serious enough to contact police, it's serious enough for tow trucks to arrive). Tow trucks will be called by the police — this is not your responsibility. You are responsible, however, for informing the tow-truck driver where you would like your vehicle taken. Don't let him or her select a shop. Instead, have it removed to your mechanic or dealership. If you don't have a mechanic you prefer to work with, you can always have your car transported to a different shop after a few days. It will be some time before any work is started.

You'll need to contact your insurance agent within at least one business day of the accident. All too often consumers wash their hands of the process once the insurance company has taken over. This is not a good idea. Keep control over what is happening to your vehicle. Don't let someone else decide what will be done with your assets without your approval.

The insurance adjuster will prepare an estimate of parts and costs to repair the car, usually in conjunction with the appraiser employed by the body shop. Make sure to ask your insurance adjuster if repairs are to be completed with new or replacement (used) parts.

If the estimate for repairs does not exceed the replacement value of your vehicle, then repair work will begin. If the repair estimate exceeds the replacement value, then the insurance company will not repair your car. This is called a "write-off." It's less expensive for the insurance company to buy you a replacement vehicle than it is to repair your old one.

Some discrepancies can occur at this point if you aren't watching carefully. First, the replacement value of your car is based on its black book value at the time of the accident. Find out the black book value of your car, and appeal the insurance company's choice of replacement value if you feel you are being wronged. A good example of such a case involved a woman whose 1988 Nissan Sentra was involved in a front-end collision in Toronto in early 1996. Her car was valued at $3000. The damage was severe enough that the car was a borderline write-off. The insurance company did not know, however, that the car should have been valued higher than the black book wholesale price. The woman had invested several thousand dollars in brake and exhaust work only three months before the accident. A write-off would not have allowed her to recoup the car's true value.

If you don't want your car to be written off, you have several choices.

- You can appeal the repair estimate to your adjuster. Ask another body shop to provide an estimate.

- You can choose to use replacement (used) parts instead of new ones.

- You can offer to pay the difference between the repair estimate and the replacement value of the car.

Whatever you decide, make sure that you are fully advised of everything that is happening with your car. Is it being stored inside or outside in the days before repair work begins? Damaged metal will begin to rust when exposed to the elements. Once rust gets into your car, it's like a cancer that can never be eradicated. Visit your car and view the damage yourself. While you're there, remove all valuables and personal possessions from inside the car.

Finally, carefully inspect the repair work when you get the car back. Your insurance company has paid for this work, and your premiums will likely increase as a result. Make sure you are happy with the results.

Appendix

This appendix contains resources that may be of help to new- and used-car buyers. Most public libraries contain vast amounts of automotive information that can be easily searched and consulted. Here are some of the resources to look for.

MAGAZINES

AUTOMOBILE MAGAZINE

This is an excellent source of information, but the magazine is geared towards enthusiasts instead of the general public. You will find well-written articles about new cars in this magazine, but you're also likely to find articles about great places to drive your car. Other publications provide more definitive articles.

AUTO TRADER AND AUTO MART MAGAZINE

These publications don't offer much by way of editorial material on the range of cars available in Canada, but they are excellent sources of information on new and used cars for sale. The majority of the ads in these magazines are for pre-owned vehicles, anywhere from six months to sixty years old. *Auto Trader* magazine is divided into several different categories: European, Japanese, Domestics, Trucks, Boats, Bikes, and RVs. *Auto Trader* magazines advertise over 750 000 vehicles being sold by dealers, private individuals, and used-car lots every year.

CAR AND DRIVER MAGAZINE

This is an American publication, so make sure you get current prices from a Canadian dealer. Thankfully, the vehicles produced for the U.S. market don't differ much from Canadian ones, so information in the publication is mostly accurate in Canada. You'll find road tests of new vehicles, long-term tests of selected cars and trucks, and breaking news about new products and recalls and safety features. The "Road Test Digest" (found in the back 10 to 15 pages of each issue) outlines the issues that specific cars were tested and reported on, so that you can find information on the exact cars you're looking at.

CARGUIDE MAGAZINE

One of two Canadian automotive publications, published every two months. Information is based on Canadian vehicles with Canadian prices. You'll also find news in this magazine on buying trends that are based on the Canadian market.

CONSUMER REPORTS

Each issue usually contains some information on specific cars—often a comparison test. As well, the April issue each year is the annual *Auto Issue,* with ratings, profiles, reliability ratings, and crash-test results. This magazine prides itself on being completely independent of manufacturers and dealers. In fact, *Consumer Reports* actually *buys* all the vehicles it tests. As a result, the magazine does not cover every car that is available (it's just too expensive), but you know the information on the cars that are included is completely unbiased.

MOTOR TREND

If you're a performance car enthusiast, this is the magazine that will provide you with the most cutting edge information about the world of sports cars. Although the magazine editors do occasionally review sedans, the majority of their articles are about road-worthy speed machines. This magazine is also a U.S. publication, so make sure to convert the prices you read to Canadian dollars.

POPULAR MECHANICS CAR SMART MAGAZINE

Although this is a relatively new auto magazine, it's an excellent publication geared more towards the consumer than towards the automobile fanatic. The articles not only deal with road tests of many different types of cars, but also give shopping tips, comparisons between leasing and financing, and more. This is an American publication, so prices are in U.S. dollars. The March issue is the annual *New Car & Truck Buyer's Guide,* with ratings on all cars and trucks available in North America.

ROAD & TRACK MAGAZINE

The venerable competitor with *Car and Driver*, it's often hard to differentiate between the two magazines. Although they rarely disagree on a particular car, it's useful to consult road tests from both magazines because one will usually contain more detailed information than the other. Again, this is a U.S. publication, so prices are different from what you'll find on this side of the border. The Road Test summary at the back of the magazine lists issues that include specific vehicle reports.

WORLD OF WHEELS

Another Canadian magazine, published six times a year. This magazine is often distributed free with some Thomson newspapers. The information is usually not as in depth as you'll find in *Carguide*.

These are just a few of the magazines you'll find in libraries and bookstores. The automotive industry is so diversified that you'll find a large number of specialty magazines that deal with everything from custom cars to pick-up trucks to British sports cars.

TORONTO STAR WHEELS

Although not a magazine, this is a weekly publication about cars in Canada that is an indispensable tool for any Canadian looking to buy a car. *The Toronto Star* publishes its Wheels section every Saturday. In it you'll find reviews of new cars, technology updates, used-cars reports, servicing tips, used-car classifieds, and much more. All information is Canadian.

BOOKS

THE CANADIAN RED BOOK

Wholesale and retail valuations for used cars. This is an essential resource if you're buying a pre-owned vehicle.

THE LEMON-AID GUIDES

These guides to new and used cars by Phil Edmonston are the long-standing bibles of Canadian automotive guides. The information in these books is well researched, but is sometimes outdated. The *Used Car Guide* is the better of the two publications.

The New Car Report

This Canadian book (produced in Quebec) by Jacques Duval with Denis Duquet and Marc Lachapelle is excellent both in terms of its editorial content and its photographs. This book is also sold in the United States, which is odd because it is based only on Canadian vehicles. The book is designed more for the enthusiast than the consumer, but is packed with excellent information. If you buy only one (other) car guide, this is the one to choose.

Consumer Reports Buying Guide

This book is written in the United States by the editors of *Consumer Reports* books and deals specifically with cars available for sale south of our border. The used-car version of this guide is a good shopping tool—it includes frequency of repair charts for hundreds of older vehicles. The data is compiled through actual owner surveys. Refer to this publication for quality information about used-car reliability. Again, because it's a U.S. publication, the prices are out of whack with Canada's.

Consumer Guide—Rating the Autos

This is a U.S. publication written by the editors of *Consumer Guide* magazine. The *Consumer Guide* books are full of great facts and figures, but the editorial material often reads like it's straight out of a brochure supplied by the manufacturer. The bar graph ratings they often use are great visual representations of a car's overall reliability, and perhaps the best feature of their books.

There are plenty more books available for car buyers, but the majority of them are from the United States. You'll find dozens of books covering everything from used-car-buying strategies to insurance to secret warranties. The problem with U.S. publications is that they often quote prices, equipment, and state legislation, none of which is applicable to Canadians. If you're ever in doubt about any of the information you are reading in a book, check the publishing information on the inside front pages to determine the country of origin and the age of the book.

WEBSITES

On the Internet, you'll find hundreds of different automotive websites. Every manufacturer maintains its own web presence, and you'll also find websites designed by salespeople, dealerships, enthusiasts, consumer protection agencies, and more. Because websites change often, we've decided against publishing web addresses in this book. Visit the authors' website, *www.ableauto.com*, for an up-to-date list of sites.

Index

Looking for more information on buying and selling cars?

Check out the AbleAuto web site **http://www.ableauto.com** the authors' official home page.

Mel Wise and Kendrew Pape are available for seminars anywhere in Canada!

Seminar topics include:

LEASING 101. This seminar is an in-depth look at leasing, with information about how to lease a new or used car, the common pitfalls to avoid, the best value lease deals available, the pros and cons of independent leasing houses, and more.

LEASING VS. BUYING. This seminar addresses the decades-old question: "Should I buy or lease my next car?" The seminar includes information about the advantages and disadvantages of different purchase options, including leasing, financing, direct purchase, bank financing, and more.

HOW TO NEGOTIATE. This seminar teaches participants how to become an effective negotiator for new or used cars. Learn the secrets of dealership negotiating strategies and how to counteract them. The seminar includes strategies for buying and selling new and used cars, leasing, telephone negotiating, and more.

For more information on these seminars and others, contact Vorg Inc. at 1-800-694-8674.

Kendrew Pape is the Vice-President, Marketing, of Pape Enterprises, a family communications business headed by financial writer Gordon Pape. Kendrew is a prolific automotive journalist, with two previous books to his credit and a monthly review of the automotive industry published on the AbleAuto web site. He has satiated his love for cars in many ways, including working as a car salesman and becoming involved in amateur racing. In his spare time, Kendrew enjoys writing fiction about cars, and is currently working on a 100-year anthology of automotive poetry. Kendrew studied English Literature at the University of Western Ontario.

Mel Wise is a second-generation car man. His father, Samuel Wise, was president of Allied Motor Sales, which operated from 1939 to 1959. Following in his father's footsteps, Mel joined the automobile industry in his early 20's. Since then, Mel has held a variety of positions, including general manager of Budget Rent-a-Car (Toronto) and CEO of Canada's first publicly-traded leasing company, Lease Rite, Inc. Over the past two years, Mel has teamed up with Gordon and Kendrew Pape to publish two books on buying cars in Canada. Mel brought his 30 years of automobile experience to the books, helping to shed new light on the Canadian automobile industry.